Growing Up Pentecostal

Growing Up Pentecostal

A Memoir

BY

Phil Matarese

FOREWORD BY

Philip C. Baisley

AFTERWORD BY

Jane Materese

RESOURCE *Publications* · Eugene, Oregon

Resource Publications
An Imprint of Wipf and Stock Publishers
199 W. 8th Ave., Suite 3
Eugene, OR 97401

www.wipfandstock.com

PAPERBACK ISBN: 979-8-3852-6676-0
HARDCOVER ISBN: 979-8-3852-6677-7
EBOOK ISBN: 979-8-3852-6678-4

VERSION NUMBER 01/23/26

Dedicated to all seekers,
Those who have lived the examined life,
And those who are just awaking to new realities.
May God guide you on the path as you walk in the light.

More personally,
I dedicate this book to my family, especially Jane and J,
Rebecca, Mom and Curtis (I hope you don't hate this book),
And to all of God's people I have been blessed to call
my church family throughout the years!

Contents

Foreword

MIKE PETTIT, IN THE opening paragraph of his memoir, *Raised by Wolves*, declares that his story is

> all true to the extent that I can tell the truth. It's my story, and I'm sticking to it.[1]

When I began writing *Tales of a Canarsie Boy*, my own memoir of growing up a fundamentalist Protestant in a half-Jewish, half-Italian neighborhood in Brooklyn, I let Pettit's words guide me. I didn't try to reproduce news stories, fact-checked and certified true. I wrote my recollections—the feelings, motivations, actions, and reflections of my early life.

Phillip Matarese writes that kind of memoir. He admits that his story is true to the extent that he remembers it, but he backs up his lack of guaranteed veracity with snippets of emotion, of doubt, and even of wonder at how the religious community with which he parted ways two decades ago still informs him today, for better or for worse.

I know the feeling. Although I was raised in the kind of church that believed Pentecostals were playing fast and loose with the Holy Spirit, we still fought the same battles against "principalities and powers," against "modernism," and against vices like drinking, smoking, card playing, and the movies. Many of us survived our upbringing only by renouncing it and, often, renouncing God in the process. Phil Matarese didn't. He survived by remembering his past and renewing his commitment to a God whose grace cannot be limited to the dogma of a church or a system of theology.

Reading Phil's memoir is not just a reminder of a fundamentalist past; it's an invitation to wrestle with our own. What doctrines and practices

---

1. Pettit, *Raised by Wolves*, 4.

formed us as children? Where and how did questions and doubts creep in as we progressed through our teens? When and why did the break, if there was one, occur? What remains?

For Phil Matarese, a lot remains, and even though he doesn't see eye to eye with the faith that formed him, he is grateful for it. Again, I know the feeling. I hear the echoes of my spiritual upbringers in churches and on social media today. I cringe at some of it. And then I remember the people in the pews around me, their faithfulness at worship, their work in the community, even the parties they hosted for us kids in the most conservative Christian fashion. Even though I'm happy to see a lot of my early beliefs fallen by the wayside, I'm glad I never lost the path.

Growing Up Pentecostal is not everyone's biography. It is, however, the story of one person's wrestling with a religious system that at times comforted, at times condemned, and often confused him. In spite of it, and because of it, Phillip's faith grew. In that sense, it may be your story too.

Phil Baisley

Professor of Pastoral Ministry (retired)
Earlham School of Religion
Richmond, Indiana

Acknowledgments

THANK YOU FIRST OF all to my wife, Jane, for all your encouragement and support. I'm glad we can cheer each other on in our writing and other endeavors. I appreciated your suggestions. Others who were helpful with comments, ideas, and suggestions were Phil Baisley and Steve Vachon (feedback used to write the epilogue).

Thank you to those who have mentored me in some way or another in recent years. This includes Phil Baisley and Steve Vachon, as well as Dan Bair, Dave Bell, Ryan Braught, Marilyn Drudge, Karen Duhai, Todd Hammond, Gene Hollenberg, Cindy Ploughe, Dan Poole, Kevin Whitmore, and really all the professors I had at Bethany Theological Seminary and Earlham School of Religion, as well as all the ministers and lay leaders I have worked with. It would take too long to name you all. Of course, none of you knew I was writing a book, except for Phil because I asked him a few questions about writing/publishing and later asked him to write the foreword for this book. Even Steve didn't know when we had that conversation that it was going to become a part of the book (and neither did I).

This book wouldn't have been possible without the good people of Wipf and Stock. Thanks for answering all my questions; as a first-time author, I had many.

Also, a special thanks to Michael Almquist for help figuring out permissions for the Mewithoutyou song I quoted. Who knew song copyrights were so complicated?

Lastly, thank you everyone who is reading this book. You're the reason it exists!

Introduction

> But speaking the truth in love, we must grow up in every way
> into him who is the head, into Christ, from whom the whole
> body, joined and knit together by every ligament with which
> it is equipped, as each part is working properly, promotes the
> body's growth in building itself up in love.

—EPHESIANS 4:15–16

GROWING UP PENTECOSTAL is my coming-of-age story, it's a memoir, and it's a spiritual autobiography. In seminary I wrote my spiritual autobiography at least twice; I'm sure students at other seminaries have done similar assignments. I never thought I'd write the long version of that assignment into full book form. Yet I knew I had some stories to tell, stories that were unusual, outside of the Christian norm. What do I mean by that? Simply that I had experiences much different from your average evangelical Protestant. I'm not necessarily trying to say Pentecostals or charismatics are weird. (Then again, aren't we all weird in our own way?) The kind of events described in this book are very different from my more traditional Anabaptist faith that I found as an adult and completely different from my liturgical worship from my college days. (This in itself was my reaction to growing up Pentecostal. It's funny how the original Pentecostals were rebels for how they completely changed church from the way it was in traditional denominations. I guess the way a Pentecostal college kid becomes a rebel is to have a Lutheran period.) As a child, my church experience was very unique. I won't say that it was bad, but not everything was good, as you'll read in these pages. (Is anyone's childhood all good? I doubt it.) Being a kid is hard. People always say it's easy to be a kid and not have any responsibilities. Sure, I get the argument, but when you're a kid you don't have much agency. No one asks your opinion. You do what you're told and if you don't like it, too bad. Of course, it takes time to even figure out what you like and what you don't. The same kid who likes dancing down the aisle in charismatic worship one day can grow up to find such things silly and emotional. We change with time and that's all right, and that's just one simple example. There are any number of things a child accepts uncritically that with age will be rejected or at the very least examined, beliefs modified. Do I really want to dance in church? What about speaking in tongues? How do I feel about healing? All manner of such ecstatic worship will need to be considered in this volume. I suppose it would be no different in any other kind of church: Should I cross myself? Will I pray the rosary? Should I take Communion? When should I—or should I—get baptized? Children of all types of faith will have to answer these questions when they are ready. Your parents choose which faith, or no faith, with which to raise you, and as you grow up you decide what to keep, what to tweak, and what to discard. It's not always a straight line or a clear path. Many seekers spend large portions of their lives trying to figure it out. Some people change their entire religion, rather than just denomination or congregation. The changes can be huge, yet some people don't make any changes and almost seem to uncritically accept everything their parents and religious leaders taught them: the unexamined life. Jean-Paul Sartre, writing on existentialism, says that mock feeling and true feeling are almost indistinguishable. When someone wants to consult a priest, they go to a priest with some sense of what advice that priest will give, whether as a priest that will collaborate with you, or as one that is just marking time (or going through the motions, just there to earn their paycheck), or as one among those who are resisters within their institutions.[1] In the same way, I think people are employing mock feeling when they decide not to choose for themselves, giving away their religious agency, their will to choose, and leaving it to their parents. To me this is most common in evangelical forms of Christianity and, of course, Catholic, the kind of Christianity Sartre was raised in and rejected along with all religion as he became an atheist. Obviously, some Catholics and evangelicals do make a conscious choice to remain in the church they were raised in. (It's not just Anabaptists and mainline Protestants who are thinking for themselves; that kind of generalization would be just as false as claiming all

1. Sartre, "Existentialism," 284–85.

evangelicals and Catholics uncritically accept the religion they were taught from the cradle. This is simply an observation.)

I'm going to tell you some strange stories in this book about being raised Pentecostal, but then I chose other expressions of Christianity for myself. The majority of the names in this book have been changed to protect privacy, as well as some personal details. This is not a complete retelling of every significant phenomenal church event. There were some stories I chose not to tell for fear of them being too personal for the people involved. My own personal stories are in here, and I decided not to worry about embarrassing myself, as a certain amount of vulnerability seems to be required to write a memoir. Just like when I wrote spiritual autobiography in seminary, it can be deeply personal and include things you're not proud of that show your imperfections. Choosing to share personal stories always requires risk, it would be so much easier to write a journalistic or anthropological book that would only report on what other people are doing or have done in the past. I never realized how unhealthy I was psychologically as a child through my young adult years. Writing this was somewhat therapeutic as I was forced to think about things I hadn't thought about in years, some of which I never took the time to process until now. Mental health was never much of a focus in the Pentecostal church, at least in my experience; you were just supposed to pray yourself to wellness and have the devil cast out of you. Name it and claim it, "calleth those things which be not as though they were" (Rom 4:17 KJV). Nobody ever said you should see a counselor, get some therapy, maybe take an antidepressant. I still find myself avoiding doctors, therapists, and medication—even though I think those are all good things that can help. I've worked through a lot on my own, or I thought I had, but after writing all this it seems like I might have a lot further to go.

Another choice I made as an author was to rely solely on my own memories and recollections. I considered interviewing family members for their take on events that happened but ultimately decided not to. I'm not sure how this book will be received by family and other people in the story. I have no intention of harming anyone, but if anyone is upset by this book, then I want all the blame to fall on me. The risk of relying only on my memory is that memory is imperfect. Consider what Bertrand Russell says about memory and intuitive judgements in *The Problems of Philosophy*:

when memory of something is both vivid and recent it is reliable and trustworthy.[2] Russell says,

> If the house next door was struck by lightning half a minute ago, my memory of what I saw and heard will be so reliable that it would be preposterous to doubt whether there had been a flash at all. And the same applies to less vivid experiences, so long as they are recent. I am absolutely certain that half a minute ago I was sitting in the same chair in which I am sitting now. Going backward over the day, I find things of which I am quite certain, other things of which I am almost certain, other things of which I can become certain by thought and by calling up attendant circumstances, and some things of which I am by no means certain. I am quite certain that I ate my breakfast this morning, but if I were as indifferent to my breakfast as a philosopher should be, I should be doubtful. As to the conversation at breakfast, I can recall some of it easily, some with an effort, some only with a large element of doubt, and some not at all. Thus there is a continual gradation in the degree of self-evidence of what I remember, and a corresponding gradation in the trustworthiness of my memory.[3]

He goes on to say that memory has degrees of self-evidence and trustworthiness; there are gradations in the quality of memory.[4] So, I will do my best to accurately relate these events as best I can, knowing that I'll probably get some things wrong and that is inevitable. Hopefully, there will be nothing more than minor errors; if anyone remembers something differently, I'm open to correction. If the text is to be amended that will have to wait until if and when there is a second printing. Or perhaps in the future I would consider a second book on this topic that incorporates interviews. It depends on the reception of this work and the interest level. Personally, now that I'm writing this introduction last, I'm quite ready to write about something else. One appreciates variety in topics; indeed, as the saying goes, variety is the spice of life.

It is also my intention to tell this story as respectfully as I can. I'm not Pentecostal or charismatic, and I feel like I have baggage from my upbringing. (Don't we all?) I considered writing this book forever ago, but I'm glad I waited until now. I don't think I would have been mature enough to have written respectfully when the idea first occurred to me. I'd thought of it as

2. Russell, *Problems of Philosophy*, 115–16.

3. Russell, *Problems of Philosophy*, 116.

4. Russell, *Problems of Philosophy*, 116–18.

a way of deconstructing my childhood religion, and certainly that is an unavoidable element in this retelling. However, a younger, angrier me wouldn't have cared who was hurt and wouldn't have considered the perspective of others, would not have been as concerned with objectivity—I might have even made fun of things and people I disagreed with. I'm mature enough now to avoid those pitfalls. At least I hope that's what I did.

I believe the church people I grew up with were sincere and had good intentions. I don't accuse them of being fake or having malicious intent. That said, there are certainly moments where I'm critical, but I have tried to limit that to only when necessary. There are Pentecostals and charismatics who are worthy of criticism. This book is not about them, but I'll give you two examples anyway. One easy example that most readers probably already have in mind are televangelists and faith healers. No, I won't name names. There are plenty of sources you can find for yourself on the subject, and I invite you to explore the topic if it interests you. I make occasional reference to these folks as is relevant to my personal narrative. Another example I'll give you is a personal one about people using prophecy for their own ends—false prophets who tell you what you want to hear (1 Kgs 22:8, 2 Tim 4:3). That happened to Jane and me, not long after we got married. We were trying to get pregnant and were just starting to realize that it wasn't going to be as easy as we thought (actually, it wasn't even possible, but we didn't know that yet). There was a group of church folks from some sort of Pentecostal or charismatic church, and they were proselytizing in the Walmart parking lot by going on a spiritual scavenger hunt, looking for people to pray for. According to one guy, he was looking for someone in a Red Lion T-shirt. Lucky me, I was wearing my ancient Red Lion baseball community league T-shirt that I almost never wore. He asked if there was anything they could pray with us about. I had my doubts, but Jane, who was probably more desperate than I was (and more open-minded), shared that we were trying to get pregnant and were having difficulty. As they prayed for us, one woman said she saw Jane becoming pregnant and having a little girl. Jane was smart and tried to test the prophecy by asking the woman if she knew what the child's name would be, after some hesitation, she said something with a J. We did in fact have a name that began with J picked out for a girl. So, we thought, okay, maybe these people aren't a bunch of phonies. Of course, Jane starts with a J, as do many popular names, so lucky guess is what I say now—say the name or it doesn't count. But the fact of the matter is, they told us what we wanted to hear in hopes that we would come to their church. We already had a church we liked just fine, and my background of growing up Pentecostal and intentionally leaving it for more traditional denominations didn't make me very likely to want to go back to a new one. Who knows, maybe we would have thought we owed them if the prophecy had come true. But these people were full of it, and I'm not referring to the Holy Spirit. People like these false prophets I have no problem with saying negative comments about and denouncing. I don't know if anything comparable ever took place at my childhood church. If it did, I can't remember. We had prophecy all the time, but I have forgotten 99 percent of it. The only prophecy I remember the content of came from a visiting minister couple who said I would grow up to be a pastor (I am in fact a pastor). At the time, as a small child, I thought, how about a baseball player instead? Who wants to be a pastor? But here we are. No, I don't know if they really saw that or if they thought, here's a good church boy, what are the odds he becomes a pastor? Probably higher than some random kid in another context, and his mom would probably like to hear that. To be clear, I'm not saying it's one or the other—a real prophecy or a let's-just-make-something-up scenario. I have no idea. This is a very hazy memory; it is not vivid and certainly not near. (Bertrand Russell would probably advise against calling them prophets or lucky guessers based on the passage I quoted earlier. He might have been fine with sharing an opinion based on his negative view of Christianity, which would be subjective rather than objective as he himself would have told you.) I don't remember the ministers' names, or if they visited our church more than once. Could they be a positive example of prophets? Well, in this instance what they said came true,[5] so they just might be for all I know, but I have no idea. Also, I don't think I really even thought about this memory at the time of my call to ministry. Maybe it was somewhere in my psyche in the back of my mind, but I didn't think about it consciously, and I didn't consider it an affirmation—I doubt very much that I considered it at all other than eventually to recall it. Too much time had elapsed; it was not a strong memory.

One more disclaimer, or word of caution seems in order before you proceed further. Taking off my pastor hat for a minute to put on my writer hat—oh, maybe the fact that I feel the need to warn you means that I'm still wearing it (oh great, now I'm the mad hatter). Music was a major influence on me in my youth. I make a fair amount of musical references. Most of them are secular, nonreligious, often of the parental advisory

5. 1 Thess 5:19–22.

variety (although they rarely had that official label because most of my music was/is indie, not mainstream). If young readers are reading, as a pastor I feel compelled to say that I am not making musical recommendations. If you're of an age to make your own decisions in such matters then I will just say that everything I reference I do still enjoy even if I no longer listen to it or have it in my music library. You can take that as an endorsement if you want, or not. Also, most of this music is old anyway; it's probably not what the kids are listening to these days, so there's that. It's funny how even for some of these bands that are still active, now they're all really old. Not that it matters, and of course, I listened to Black Sabbath, the Ramones, the Beatles, the Clash (etc.), who were all really old or in some cases had some band members who were already dead when I was listening to them as a teenager. (And so the musical references have begun—you have been forewarned. Close the book now if you're worried about all that devil music.) Chapter 5 has a lot about music, but secular rock music is referenced in other chapters too.

But why tear out single pages when you can throw away the book?[6]

(There's a Christian rock reference for you, so calm down, that's in here too). I suppose I could give you a breakdown of the other chapters, but I always hate that because when I read I'm going to read the whole book anyway unless it really sucks, or if it's assigned reading and I only need certain parts for a class, so you really don't have to tell me what each chapter is about in the introduction. It doesn't make for an interesting read; sometimes I just skim through to the end. Anyway, that's enough critique of other authors' introduction-writing style. No doubt you'll dislike something about mine, like this almost pointless rant about introductions.

This is a religious book, but it's also a book about growing up, and teenagers are weird quasi-adults—yet still children. Teenagers do and say weird things. My apologies to any teenage readers for the last sentence but admit it—it's true! I guess I'm giving you one final warning that not everything in the story of my teenage years is super Christian. Most of

---

6. Mewithoutyou, "Torches Together." Yes, if you're paying attention, you'll notice that I'm citing music as CDs in the bibliography; I have those because I'm old. Although, I usually put them on my non-updated version of iTunes on my old laptop and onto my phone, early 2000s style. Feel free to make fun of me. However, I feel like we lose something when we only have digital music—the materiality of the album, the artwork—and I literally flipped through the lyrics to make sure I quoted accurately. Yes, I'm very opinionated about such things.

my friends weren't very religious when I was in high school. Then again, I was a fairly tame teenager, but there will be some slightly off-color passages. I did, however, keep language PG and in most cases G, now that I got some people all excited—prepare for disappointment if you wanted some f-bombs or something. Wow, I told you to throw away the book, and now I'm telling you to be disappointed—not a very good way to write an introduction. Should have gone with "chapter 1 is about . . . and then in chapter 2 . . . ," etc. Maybe the publisher (assuming there is one) will edit all my nonsense out. But if not, people do often say you should laugh at yourself, so that's what I'm doing here. There's humor, but most of the time my tone is quite serious. If I didn't scare you away, please proceed. Speaking of scaring . . . chapter 1 is called "Fear of the Devil," but I said I wasn't going to do that. So without further ado . . .

Chapter 1: **Fear of the Devil**

The God of peace will shortly crush Satan under your feet.
The grace of our Lord Jesus Christ be with you.

—Romans 16:20

KIDS ARE OFTEN AFRAID of lots of things. Some are logical, like the fe-
rocious dog next door or aggressive bees like hornets, yellowjackets, and
wasps. Some fears are less logical, like the dark, clowns, or math tests. Okay,
maybe those are logical fears too, but they're abstract, yet no less a part of
our psyche. We can't necessarily explain these fears. My childhood fear was
the devil. Yeah, I say childhood fear, but really this was a fear from the age
of seven to around twenty-three. Although this is a fear that I conquered,
if I have a nightmare that isn't of the adult variety—such as the death of
a loved one or not being able to find a toilet—if a nightmare has a creepy
villain, it is more likely than not to be Satan or a demon. However, these
dreams are very rare. A more typical dream for me would be something like
this: I'm looking for a book I want to read and am interrupted by needing
to do the dishes, while an old high school friend, real or imagined, knocks
on the door, and then suddenly we're at a restaurant, but the food isn't very
good, but that's okay because now I'm the waiter, and actually, I'm not even
myself; now I'm a random dream character stuck in a boring job, but I
found that book I was looking for that a customer left on the table and now
it's mine. Basic adult nonsense—maybe the devil even makes a cameo appearance, except he'll be the customer at the next table who says this hot
sauce you brought me is so weak it should be a sin, but that doesn't mean I
like it sinful or not, nor will I give you a tip, and why is angel food the only
cake on the dessert menu? So, yeah, not particularly scary, more ridiculous

than anything. (If you're a Harry Potter fan, think of the way the kids deal with a bogart in Lupin's class as they turn their phobias into something laughable.[1]) Guess I've done all right if my old phobias are more likely to turn into a joke than cause for fright.

I had a lot of nightmares in childhood through my early twenties, which is common according to psychological research.[2] I finally got over my fears partly through my changing theology in college and a temporary ability to lucid dream. For several months I had terrible nightmares, but I got tired of it and said enough. Actually, I said it in my dream: I said, "This is just a stupid dream, and I don't have to take it. In fact, because none of this is real, I can do whatever I want, and now I think I'll just fly away." So, that's just what I did. Sometimes it was more like floating, or hovering, a little bit better than (if I can cite an old punk rock song that most of you won't know) the guy in the Vandals song that wishes he can fly, but it turns out he can only fly for a foot or two and not very high, about an inch or so.[3] (Thanks for humoring me.) Other times in my lucid dreams when I decided to fly away, I would be up in the clouds, looking down on the city. Maybe I would even fly to a new exotic location, because why not? As I often said in the dream, "This is a dream, and I can do whatever I want." That is how I got over my fear of the devil and nightmares. Sometimes I wish I could still lucid dream, because it was a lot of fun, but without the need for it, I lost the ability. I'm sure there is some psychology we could go into about that, but it is way beyond the scope of this book. I dip my toe in the waters of psychology and philosophy but I'm going to try to stay in my lane as a layman in those areas. (I like including tidbits from those fields in my sermons, where I find a little is nice, but too much loses the audience, who are more interested in stories).[4]

But let's start at the beginning, with this fear or phobia started around age seven, after my parents' divorce and after my mom had changed churches from the Assemblies of God, what I'll call the Pentecostal establishment, to an independent Pentecostal/charismatic church. I'll talk about this more in the next chapter; for now it will be sufficient to say that in this new church environment we didn't just have stories of the devil in the Bible

1. Rowling, *Harry Potter*, 130–40.

2. Pacheco and Rehman, "Nightmares in Children."

3. The Vandals, "An Idea for a Movie."

4. Jung, *Memories*. Jung has some very interesting writings about his own dreams in his autobiography, which I recommend if you find dreams intriguing.

and preaching about overcoming Satan. But now sermons included stories of battling the devil, who might visibly appear at any moment. Certainly, Pastor George might have his own stories; ironically, I don't remember any if he did. But he might include in sermons anecdotes from Smith Wigglesworth, a British Pentecostal evangelist who would cast demons out of drunks and once chased a few back into the pub after they cursed him, so he then preached to them right there in public.[5] And he would heal people by hitting them in the affected area, even punching people in the stomach for stomach and gastrointestinal issues. When asked why he hit people, he said he didn't hit them, he hit the devil who was causing the ailment.[6] He also had a story about waking up one night feeling an evil presence, seeing Satan, and Smith said, oh, it's just you, rolled over, and went back to sleep.[7] Now, as an adult relating these stories in a memoir, I see the humor in them, and I guess to Pentecostals such as my mom and Pastor George, these stories were badass. You can defeat the devil and laugh at him too. I also remember a testimony from Ben, one of the deacons at our church, who said he woke up at night and saw Satan, and he was complaining about how he was failing to get to Ben and his family (kind of has Screwtape vibes).[8] The last example I'll put out there I remember from a sermon from one of the televangelists my mom watched (we'll leave him anonymous): he related a time when the devil appeared in his rearview mirror while he was driving and tried to scare him. By the way, thanks a lot to that guy, when I was a new driver, if I was out at night, sometimes I didn't want to look in my rearview mirror, just in case. It's kind of like that Bloody Mary myth, that if you say her name three times she'll appear in a mirror. Don't even get me started on that—I would always try not to think of that urban legend any time I was around mirrors. (Will she appear if you only think her name, even if you did it by accident? I didn't want to find out.) But that's not quite the devil, or is it?

This is the environment I was in as a young child, hearing stories of supernatural phenomena. Almost like Christian ghost stories, the paranormal recounted on a daily basis like it was no big deal. Of course, it wasn't just the devil we would hear about; people saw Jesus and angels too, but they weren't scary, so they didn't capture the child's imagination in

5. Wigglesworth, *Greater Works*, 515; Wilson, *Smith Wigglesworth*, 48–49.

6. Wigglesworth, *Only Believe*, 9–11; Wilson, *Smith Wigglesworth*, 74–75.

7. Wilson, *Smith Wigglesworth*, 123–24.

8. Lewis, *Screwtape Letters*.

quite the same way—you didn't have to worry about them. But all of these stories were told in a matter-of-fact way. You could hear it in a sermon recounted from an old-time evangelist or from someone's own personal experience. Angels and demons were around every corner. But we had our standards; everything in moderation, as the apostle Paul says (Phil 4:5 KJV). I remember one of my mom's customers for her housecleaning business was a charismatic Catholic, and my mom said if she had a stain in her couch that wouldn't come out she would try to cast the demon out of her couch. Being the cleaning expert and Pentecostal intercessor that she was, Mom thought this woman was being ridiculous and just needed better stain remover. She said it came from her reading a book called *Pigs in the Parlor*.[9] Apparently, this book encouraged paranoia about demons being everywhere, even hiding in your couch cushions it would seem. I guess there's always someone who is a little more out in left field. Personally, I didn't mind that lady; she didn't have those conversations with me if I was there with my mom during the summer or when I was pretending to be sick and got sent home from school, she had a really cool fat brown dog that loved kids, and she had cable (we didn't have that at home) so I could watch cartoons. Sure beats *The Price Is Right* and talk shows.

The devil was real, and I heard more about him than I would have cared to. I guess after a while it just added up until he/it became this terrifying entity. It wasn't long before I had my own encounters.

At this time Mom, my sister Rebecca, and I were living in our first apartment after the divorce. Prior to that we had lived with church friends, stayed short-term with a family from the Assemblies of God church, and had a somewhat longer stay with one of Mom's friends from the same church who was also going through a divorce and who then discovered our new church along with us. In the apartment, I had the larger upstairs bedroom, but that was where the perks of my room ended. The floors were old hardwood that needed refinishing. The lighting wasn't good—it was always dimly lit at best. Mom also told me when I was older that Deacon Daryl found a crack pipe under the radiator when church friends were helping us move in. So, I had the dark, creepy, crack-smoking room. The setting was ripe for scaring a seven-year-old going through family trauma on top of all the supernatural stories I was hearing. The first time I thought I saw the devil I am now most convinced was nothing. I remember waking up, probably from a nightmare, and was already on my journey to Mom's room

9. Hammond and Hammond, *Pigs in the Parlor*.

4

when I thought I saw a disembodied cartoon-esque face with a baseball cap. Really, I think as I was moving from the dark room to the lighted hallway, the changing light played tricks on my eyes as they were adjusting to the light, probably partly shut, already in a state of terror. Once I thought I saw something, it was just like one of those stories from church. So, I had to run to Mom's room and wake her up. This became a habit that lasted way too long, even into my preteen years. Eventually, I came up with my own coping methods, reading books, playing video games, watching movies, basically anything but sleep. I had bad insomnia in my teen years; it's no wonder I did poorly in school. Of course, lack of sleep was only part of that equation. Of course, poor sleep habits can also cause nightmares.

The second time I saw the devil is the only instance of seeing a supernatural being that I still question, because it was the most real, and I can still picture it in my mind more clearly than any of the other incidents. This was probably a few months after the first "sighting." I don't remember why, but I was not in my room. Either I was coming back from Mom's room if I was sent back, or I was coming from Rebecca's room—sometimes we all slept in her room because she didn't sleep well either. So, Mom and I would have sleeping bags, and it would be a slumber party. Maybe I was coming from the bathroom. I don't really remember. At some point I stopped using my room as much as possible, but it was probably after this incident. Anyway, I was coming back from wherever I was and I looked across the lit hallway towards my dark room and saw a hooded figure, short, no face visible, in a dark red or brown robe. It looked a little similar to the Tusken raiders or Sand People in the first *Star Wars* movie (I hadn't seen *Star Wars* until maybe five years later, so it wasn't from watching that) or honestly (this will sound much less creepy) it looked even more like the dinks from *Spaceballs* who are a parody of the Sand People—but as I said without a face, yikes. So, I ran as fast as I could to wherever Mom was, and I never slept in my room in that apartment again.

In my college years when I was deconstructing my faith and beliefs, I had a period where I didn't believe in Satan or demons at all. It had all been a figment of my imagination from paranoia created in a world of angels and demons in constant cosmic battle, symbols and metaphors that were brought to life by people who took things too literally. A good example of taking angels and demons as nonliteral beings is explained in Tillich's *Systematic Theology*. He writes,

The truth of the doctrine of angelic and demonic powers is that there are supra-individual structures of goodness and supra-individual structures of evil. Angels and demons are mythological names for constructive and destructive powers of being, which are ambiguously interwoven and which fight with each other in the same person, in the same social group, and in the same historical situation. They are not beings but powers of being dependent on the whole structure of existence and involved in the ambiguous life. Man is responsible for the transition from essence to existence because he has finite freedom and because all dimensions of reality are united in him.[10]

As my view was similar to Tillich's at the time,[11] I was then able to dismiss this encounter as nothing more than a childhood delusion. For years I was satisfied with that explanation. The problem is, I didn't stay the skeptical universalist[12]—theologically almost Unitarian. That was just a phase for part of my college years, as I made my way back to a centered orthodox Christianity. Although I don't see much purpose in a demon appearing just to scare a little boy, it's theoretically possible. What eventually convinced me that Satan exists is the reality of evil, the holocaust, the gulag, genocide, mass shootings, etc. I don't think humans are that bad on their own. Now does that mean there are little red creatures with horns, a tail, a pitchfork, and a pointy goatee with waxed mustache, probably not, but who knows. These are images that come out of the Middle Ages and Renaissance art, along with our images of angels: angels with wings, halos, cherubic babies, pretty ladies, and muscled yet slightly effeminate archangels with big swords. These images don't come from the Bible. In fact, Satan in Hebrew simply means the accuser.[13] Anyone can be an accuser; you don't have to be a supernatural being for that. So, I don't know, did I see some sort of being lingering from some poor, tormented drug addict that never left that depressing room? Or was it simply a trick of the mind in a scared, sleepy boy? I lean heavily towards the second explanation, but I no longer have total doubt to completely dismiss it as utter nonsense. I'll never know, and I guess that's okay. In my sermons I preach a lot about

10. Tillich, *Systematic Theology*, 40.

11. I actually really like Tillich and most of what he has to say on existentialism, even if I don't agree with him on the aforementioned point anymore.

12. It's worth noting that this is different from universal restoration, which does have biblical precedent (1 Cor 15:22). Brown, *Another Way of Believing*, 159–61.

13. Job 1:7–9.

mystery. Normally, I'm talking about something positive, the mysteries of God. Sometimes I talk about mystery in regard to the question of why bad things happen to good people. I suppose supernatural phenomena would fall under the same category. We don't know why. Did St. Anthony, according to legend, really battle demons in the desert, or did the poor guy just need a drink of water and some shade? If he did battle demons, what was the purpose?[14] Goodness knows it's challenging enough to have a vital prayer life even without demons distracting you. I guess we have smartphones, TV, and video games to do all that now; we probably wouldn't look up from our phones long enough to notice a demon standing in front of us. Maybe if we went to live out in the wilderness to devote our lives to prayer and gave up our worldly distractions, we might see some weird stuff too. Anything is possible, I suppose.

There was one other incident where I had convinced myself I had seen a demon. Similarly, I later "saw" Jesus and an angel. However, if I had a vision of Jesus, you would think I would remember it now. These three later visions happened at our next apartment when I was a little older. I think it more likely I had a dream that felt real at the time, or it was similar to the first cartoon demon, a trick of the light on sleepy eyes and a paranoid child's mind. Perhaps I also wanted to see something good for a change, so it was time for Jesus—and an angel, too, for good measure. While I am skeptical about all of my childhood encounters with supernatural beings, these last three I am certain did not happen. To be clear, I'm not discounting others having visions; this is merely a critique of what I thought I saw back then, and of how I was primed for a fright. If I hadn't been hearing so much about demons, I wonder if I would have "seen" anything—and if I had, how I would have interpreted it on my own.

Some may be wondering if others in the family had visions or encounters. As noted in the introduction, this memoir is purely my own memories and perspectives, and I'm going to leave it to my own experience. I cannot or will not comment one way or the other on anything they experienced. If I study this topic in the future and they are comfortable sharing, then I'll get their stories. For now, you'll have to be content with my own anecdotes and those I share of others whose names and personal details have been changed. We'll leave it at the fact that I was in an environment where the supernatural was experienced daily within the faith community. What they did or did not see I cannot say for certain, other

14. Ward, *Sayings of the Desert*, 1–7; Athanasius, *Life of Anthony*.

than to relate the stories that were told. I won't make any judgments as to whether it was real, I can only speculate on my own encounters. No doubt many of the congregants have since had their own thoughts on what they remember from this time. Maybe some are still seeing into the spirit realm at another dimensional level. True, it is my own inclination to doubt, but I leave space for mystery, the things that can't be explained. Who am I to say what is real for someone else. We each perceive our world in our own unique way, different from anyone else's perspective.

As for my own experience, I continued in existential dread, with the fear of the unknown each night. Would the devil torment me while I tried to sleep? There was always that possibility, and it was cause enough for my angst. By age nine or ten I didn't see or delude myself into a belief that I had seen anything in the spirit. But there were still dreams, the anxiety of night, and always the potential for new phenomena to fear. While the usual fear was ever present, new fears could always be introduced, like the time I went to a sleepover and saw *Nightmare on Elm Street*. Then dreams were even scarier, because what if Freddy Krueger or something like him could be real and kill me in my dream. Then there was the time I saw an episode of *Are You Afraid of the Dark* about vampires, and then I was looking over my shoulder for them too, at least whenever I was in a dark room. I slept with the light on for most of childhood. I finally started sleeping with the light out in my early twenties, and I did that gradually, usually by leaving the TV on so there would be additional light. Often, I would use the Catholic channel so there would be something comforting if I woke up from a nightmare. By this point I was disillusioned by televangelists, so the Catholic channel was the best available Christian option.

There is a specific incident I remember when I was around twelve years old. Rachel, a friend of ours, told me and my sister Rebecca a story about a woman who experienced the stigmata while praying. Of course, she didn't know the word stigmata that we can read about in the biography of St. Francis.[15] But she told us about how this holy woman, while praying, was bleeding from her hands, feet, and side, just like Jesus in the crucifixion (that's what stigmata means): "marks appearing on the body in the places corresponding to Christ's passion wounds."[16]

Later that night I couldn't sleep. I was worried that I too might be given the stigmata. Obviously, I wasn't connecting it with holiness; it

15. Okey, *Little Flowers*, 87–112; Bonaventure, *Life of St. Francis*, 306–14.

16. McKim, *Westminster Dictionary*, 305.

sounded much more like a punishment to me, or like something the devil would do to mess with good Christians. Here, have some nail marks in your hands since you love Jesus so much! Why the devil should have the power to do such a thing I have no idea. But when anything is possible in the spirit realm it's only prudent to be afraid of it. So, that night I couldn't or wouldn't sleep, and I must have woken Mom up several times to say I was afraid, because she eventually called Elder Bob and he actually came out to our house, the first trailer we had moved into after the second apartment. Bob wanted to know why I kept waking up my mother and what I was so afraid of. I then, probably with much embarrassment, sheepishly related the story Rachel told about the stigmata. Elder Bob assured me that her story was a bunch of nonsense[17] and that I should go to sleep and quit bothering my mother. There was some reassurance in that, and I believe I was able to let it go after this intervention. But I was still a little worried about the stigmata, just in case, because you never know. Not the sort of thing you want to take you by surprise.

I realize in this retelling that I was paranoid about a lot of things throughout my childhood and adolescence. The problem with a vibrant and active spirit realm was the endless possibilities for all kinds of supernatural phenomena. Consider this: prophecy was very real in our church. Whenever Pastor George was getting a word from the Lord, I was always a little worried that he would point to me and call out some sin, real or perceived (I won't say imagined), and cast the devil out of me. Surly, there weren't any demons in me. I was so afraid of the devil, you would think I would know if I was possessed, but what if I was and I didn't know? Or what if Pastor George said I was guilty of sin or had a demon but was wrong? What if he saw a demon and it was just there hanging out in church, and he thought it was mine? There was always some anxiety during the prophetic portion of the service. In fairness, I don't think Pastor George ever had any prophecy about me in any memorable way. If ever he did, it was something basic and innocuous, because I don't remember anything dramatic. But I was convinced Pastor George could read minds—sure it was the Holy Spirit talking to him, but he could read minds too, I was certain of it—and if he could do it then so could other people, right? Pastor George wouldn't be the only one, and why should it just be pastors that had this ability? I remember, even in high school, worrying about people reading my mind.

17. To my Catholic friends, I really like St. Francis. I'm just relaying Elder Bob's sentiments here.

If I was having a controversial thought, I would try to stifle it by thinking of music. And while I was at it, I might as well make it something cool, like a good punk rock song. I wouldn't want my mind reader to think any less of me by having a boring old gospel song in my head. If someone is going to read my mind they might as well think, hey, at least that's a pretty cool kid. Had I read Harry Potter back then I would have thought Pastor George was a Legilimens, but I didn't read the books or watch the movies until college, because Harry Potter was evil! The witchcraft with all the brewing potions and cauldrons, owls delivering mail, flying broomsticks, and magic wands was just like real witches and wizards! I can't remember if Pastor George ever commented on Harry Potter; I think I have Pat Robertson to blame for this one. Thanks, Pat![18]

Yes, I had many paranoid delusions that something big and sinister was going on in my world, and the delusions were left unchecked for a long time. What I had seems to go beyond what the wise Slartibartfast would call perfectly normal paranoia (everyone in the universe has that) in *The Hitchhiker's Guide to the Galaxy*.[19] There was nothing my religious community could do about it, because no matter what they might say, all the things I was afraid of had some precedent in their world that they talked about all the time. The spirit world, both good and bad, was an ever-present reality. Best get used to it. If you're afraid, even though you're only a kid, that's your problem, because God does not give you a spirit of fear, but rather of power, love, and a sound mind.[20] All I needed to do was claim that Scripture and live into it. Easy for adults to say, but what's a kid to do? You can tell a child not to be afraid, but if you talk about scary stuff in front of them it sends mixed messages. As Karl Barth once said,

> [When] we believe too much in the strength of the devil, we bury Christ again after his resurrection.[21]

Also, maybe we needed the kid's version of Pentecostalism, but there wasn't milk for anyone; everyone got meat, even if you choked on it.[22]

18. Hananoki, "Pat Robertson Warns."

19. Adams, *Ultimate Hitchhiker's Guide*, 127.

20. 2 Tim 1:7.

21. Barth, *Faith of the Church*, 52.

22. 1 Cor 3:2: "I fed you with milk, not solid food, for you were not ready for solid food. Even now you are still not ready."

Chapter 2: **From the Pentecostal Establishment to the Charismatic Fringe**

But ye are a chosen generation, a royal priesthood, an holy nation, a peculiar people; that ye should shew forth the praises of him who hath called you out of darkness into his marvellous light.

—1 Peter 2:9 (KJV)

The church I was born into was the Assemblies of God, or what I will call the Pentecostal establishment. To add clarity, here are some actual dictionary definitions. According to Donald McKim, Pentecostalism is composed of

> movements that experience the Holy Spirit most often prominently including glossolalia, or speaking in tongues. . . . Also the several denominations arising from early 20th century revivals that stress a special baptism of the Holy Spirit after conversion.[1]

He describes the charismatic movement as

> a transdenominational movement originating in the 1950s that emphasizes the charismatic gifts of the Spirit, particularly speaking in tongues . . . words of wisdom, knowledge, healings, prophecy, and the interpretation of tongues.[2]

My childhood understanding of charismatic being a more intense version Pentecostal is incorrect. I don't know if Pastor George or others were using

1. McKim, *Westminster Dictionary*, 233.
2. McKim, *Westminster Dictionary*, 48.

it to differentiate themselves from what I called the Pentecostal establishment, or if they simply used the words interchangeably and the nuance was lost on me. Services at the Assemblies of God (AOG) were not that different from your standard protestant denomination, but there were Holy Spirit extras, like speaking in tongues and prayer lines where you might get slain in the Spirit. Most of the service was in a regular format. The music was primarily hymns and praise choruses. While there are obvious differences from non-Pentecostal or charismatic churches, there were also many similarities. A service was still fairly predictable and ordinary, just with the denominational flavor, a little extra portion of the Spirit for you. Rebecca and I were the third generation; the church was chosen by our grandparents before Mom and her siblings were born. I don't think either one of them grew up Pentecostal. Our dad grew up Catholic, but in his youth, his family changed to Assemblies of God. When Dad moved from Delaware to Pennsylvania, he met Mom at church, and an ill-conceived romance was born. Two young kids with little in common got married not long out of high school. It was a match made in purgatory. I won't be dramatic and say hell—obviously it wasn't a match made in heaven as the saying goes. They divorced when I was six and Rebecca was four. Prior to that, there were two occasions where the three of us went to stay at the women's shelter temporarily. It was a time filled with uncertainty; I only have vague memories of it. There wasn't much time between that and the end of the marriage. One night when Dad was out working night shift at the bottle factory, Mom packed up our things, leaving most of the shared possessions with Dad, taking very little for herself, and that was that. As noted in the previous chapter, we stayed briefly with one family in a very nice house, living in their basement. Then Mom's other church friend Sandra was also going through a divorce too, so it made sense for them to band together. Sandra's house was much smaller, out in the country. I remember that she had two pet goats. The nicer of the two was sometimes roaming free outside. Rebecca and I were afraid of them, even the nice one.

Initially, when Mom and Sandra became roommates, they were still going to the Assemblies of God church. Dad was asked to leave as he was harassing Mom. Shortly thereafter he rejoined the Catholic church. In the meantime, the pastor of our church moved to another congregation. We got a new pastor who was a little older and apparently less interesting; the sermons must have been dryer and less Spirit-filled. Then one day there was a tent revival that Mom and Sandra felt led to attend for various reasons, and yes, going to a tent revival was the sort of thing they would do. I'm not sure if this is still a popular thing. I did recently see a sign advertising one (and no, I did not feel led to attend, also for various reasons that you should be able to guess by this point in your reading). It seems like something out of a past era. Anyway, there was an evangelist who regularly set up the tent in our hometown during the time of year when the weather was nice, and the tent would fill up. Even if the services were long, there was lots going on, and if that got old you could see outside of the tent, watch the birds and butterflies—they might even be in the tent too. The chairs were set up in the grass, or I think sometimes over mulch, so you could pick dandelions or throw woodchips at each other: not something you can do in a church building.

While there one night, Mom and Sandra met Pastor George. Others from his congregation were there. Even Tara, the church's worship leader, was helping the evangelist's praise band. When they talked to him and learned about his church, they wanted to check it out. They were bored with the old church, it didn't seem to be fulfilling them anymore, they weren't being fed (Pentecostal vernacular), and this independent congregation that met in a hotel conference room seemed like just the thing the Spirit ordered. Rebecca and I were fine with it. This church was different. There was dancing in the aisle; you could even go to the front and run around and jump—the adults actually encouraged it. There was a lot more speaking in tongues. I don't really remember glossolalia at the AOG; I know they did it, but I don't remember ever paying any attention to it. Not only was it more prevalent, but they wanted us kids to speak in tongues too. I doubt we knew what to think of it. I remember one night, either Sunday or Wednesday, we were back in the Sunday school room with Tara, and she wanted us to learn to speak in tongues. She prayed first to show us how it was supposed to sound, then we were supposed to do it. I don't remember how long it took, but I think we caught on pretty quick and each said a few one-syllable words that we repeated. I doubt very much that this was glossolalia, but she seemed satisfied, so from that time forth we spoke in tongues. If during the service Pastor George, Tara, or someone else, asked people to pray in the Spirit, then we would join everyone else in the cacophony with our funny little words.

At our new church they also had the prayer line and even little kids were invited to come forward and get slain in the Spirit. It looked like fun to fall on the floor, so why wouldn't a kid want to join in? Did we fall down because we were touched by the Spirit or because everyone else was doing it and it looked like a good time? This far removed I can't really say. Back then and for my entire adolescence I would have sworn it was absolutely real, and we couldn't stand in the presence of the Holy Spirit. Then in college, during my deconstruction period, I would have sworn that it was all groupthink, and we behaved in the way we were expected to in that social environment. The expectation was you get hands laid on you and then you fall down. So, you fulfill people's expectations to make them happy. Now decades later it feels hard to judge one way or the other. One could give it the benefit of the doubt and say it was real, it was our experience, and why not put it in the category of faith and mystery? Then again, one could just as easily dismiss it and say I don't believe in such things. While my tendency is to fall in the second category, a generous orthodoxy[3] would leave room for the Spirit to move in such a way. Being dismissive is usually not the best approach when dealing with questions of faith and the spiritual. Also, there's no way to test it. True, I could go to a service where these practices occur, but there's no way to go back to a congregation that no longer exists, and to a past child self that has grown up into an adult with biases where the child had none. It would likely prove nothing to try and instead would only confirm my preferences for calm and orderly mainline services over free-spirited charismatic worship.

As kids we loved it, especially in the beginning before the fear started. It was just a good time. It felt like you were getting away with something being allowed to act a little crazy at church. For the moment, two quiet kids opened up a little, didn't mind being up front, and had no inhibitions. We got swept up in it as much as Mom, or at least almost. Maybe we all needed something cathartic, why not? From this first impression church became even more a central part of our lives. We had always gone to church twice on Sunday and on Wednesday evening, but now we were really focused on it. Never having been popular at school, either one of us, church became our main social center, where we had our closest friends. Rebecca became friends with Rachel, a girl the same age as me, although she was in Rebecca's grade (not the same school, that would happen later in high school). Rachel lived with her grandparents and had some behavioral issues. I became friends with Pete, Pastor George's grandson. While we were good friends, sometimes it seemed like maybe his parents invited me over to be nice. Pete was a year older, liked sports, and was tall and blonde. It didn't feel like we

3. McLaren, *Generous Orthodoxy*.

were equal peers. He was mature for his age, popular, and outgoing. I was immature for my age, quiet, and kept to myself. Pete and his older sister Tiffany babysat us sometimes; well Tiffany did, I guess Pete helped. Rachel had a huge crush on Pete that lasted as long as the church existed. It was not reciprocal. In fact, sometimes Pete distrusted me a little because I was also friends with Rachel. When Mom gave us cameras one year for Christmas (110 cameras with a small film cartridge, if that means anything to you now—Google it if you're curious), Rebecca and I took pictures of everyone and everything. Pictures of tall adults usually were cut off at the neck when we got our prints back; I guess we needed to point the camera up more. Anyway, Pete didn't want us to take his picture, which only made us want to do it even more as we chased him around the church like tiny paparazzi, flashing our cameras as he ran away with his hand over his face. Later, Mom told us Pete didn't want his picture taken because he thought we would give the pictures to Rachel. So, my alliance was sometimes in question between the two, although when we were little, he needn't have worried because I looked up to him. Besides that, I thought Rachel was kind of annoying. We mostly just tolerated each other when we were little. In a few years I would make a new church friend, Mark, a tall, thin, African American boy the same age as me. For the two years he was at church he replaced Pete as my best friend, and this time it felt reciprocal. Unfortunately, his mom remarried, and they moved to Georgia. We maintained the friendship for a few years, and he would come back occasionally for a visit. We lost contact in our teen years. We're actually friends on social media now; he has a military career. Pete and I maintained our friendship for the duration of the church's existence, but we had our ups and downs. Sometimes, I must have seemed an annoying little kid, even though we were only a year apart. I remember crying over a baseball card swap when I had let him have my best cards for unequal cards that I pretended to be okay with, so that he would like me more. But then I regretted it and felt cheated, and his parents made him give everything back and I returned his.

When the youth group was a good size, I faded into the background. When it shrunk my social capital went back up. But Pete was always the cool older kid who I would imitate—hobbies, clothes, music, haircuts. It wasn't until high school that I stopped trying to imitate him; he was a jock, and I was some sort of punk-skater-slacker friend of nerds, but see last adjective as to why I couldn't quite qualify as an actual nerd myself. I would wear the nerd label proudly now. I think my metamorphosis came when

I, influenced by Pete's music—Christian ska and punk (O.C. Supertones, Five Iron Frenzy, MxPx)—used that as a gateway to punk rock, hardcore, and metal, which aligned well with my new hobby of skateboarding. I was terrible at it but had fun. I don't think he ever got into skating. This was a hobby of my own, influenced perhaps by some of my high school friends, not Pete. I still have a guilty pleasure of listening to skate and SoCal punk. Another illustration of how I was influenced by him and took it to the next level is as follows. At this same time Pete started to spike his short hair. I did the same. Pete stopped spiking his hair and started listening to pop music, by which I mean whatever was popular on the radio. I grew my spikes out as long as I could get away with. I wanted a mohawk, but Mom wouldn't let me (that's also an AFI song[4]). I loved the first three Tony Hawk games and I got many of the CDs that had the songs on the games. I still listen to some of them: Millencolin's *Pennybridge Pioneers*, The Vandals' *Hitler Bad, Vandals Good*, Goldfinger's *Hang-Ups*, The Dead Kennedys' *Give Me Convenience or Give Me Death*, Lagwagon's *Let's Talk About Feelings*—just to name a few that I liked.

Church was my primary social scene until high school. I was still quiet and unpopular then, but I suppose I benefited from the law of averages. More people, more opportunity to make friends. However, prior to high school, church was pretty much it. Other than church friends, I often had one or two friends in elementary school, usually whoever was less popular than I was. I fared slightly better in junior high; at the end of my time there I was forming friendships that I would take into high school, but at the beginning it was more like elementary school, except in a larger crowd. So, church held a high place for me for a long time. Even in high school I already had a high regard built up all those years. Even when I had various issues, I still had respect for church and Pastor George. Though people wouldn't have taken me for a church kid by my appearance, and I was fine with that; drawing the anarchy symbol on my backpack and other places probably contributed to this perception. Not that I actually knew what anarchy was, but it looked cool and punk rock!

Church was held at such high regard that in my elementary years through junior high, our family didn't go on real/normal vacations. Instead, we went to televangelist conferences and crusades. We would go places like New York City, Washington, DC, Pittsburgh, Baltimore, Philadelphia, East Rutherford (good old New Jersey), the big cities in the mid-Atlantic.

4. AFI, "I Wanna Get a Mohawk (But Mom Won't Let Me Get One)."

Sometimes we would do a few tourist things while there. I know we went to several of the Smithsonian museums and FAO Schwarz (not that we could afford to buy anything, but it's free to look), but mostly our vacations were these healing services that filled most of the day, leaving little time for anything else. Believe me, they were long, and it was rare that we had an opportunity for sightseeing. When we were young, Rebecca and I didn't mind; this was our version of fun. I also remember that any time we got to the healing part of the service, Rebecca and I would take off our glasses, just in case we got healed. (I had glasses since the third grade, and Rebecca got glasses shortly after I did, although she recently told me that she wanted glasses too, to accessorize, so she faked her exam. Odds are she would have needed them eventually anyway, since Mom's whole family is nearsighted.) We got caught up in everything and enjoyed it right along with Mom. Of course, the summer before my first year of high school we took a trip to the beach. After that Rebecca and I were insistent upon taking the yearly beach trip; we still went to the crusades and conferences, but Rebecca and I didn't count those as vacations anymore and we asked for the beach. Mom obliged, perhaps at the cost of less of her conferences than before.

Indeed, we spent a lot of time in church, any time the doors were open—twice on Sunday, Wednesday evenings, the occasional weeklong revival with services every night (whether at our church or the tent revival). There were evangelistic events; as a kid many of the ones I was a part of involved puppets. Rebecca and I both were the main kids in the puppet show; Fran and Martha were the adults that facilitated the puppet ministry. We had a neighborhood event once in the parking lot of the White Rose Bar and Grill. We did several events at the West Manchester Mall in one of the common open spaces with lots of benches. There was also a lady who wasn't a member of our church but came sometimes, who had a ministry to inner-city kids, and we did a puppet show in her yard. Rebecca and I thought she was a little weird because she had a shofar, which is a ram's horn. She was not Jewish, yet at many Pentecostal events there always seemed to be someone who would show up with one and blow it. In our teen years, Rebecca and I called these people Jewish posers; I guess we didn't have the term cultural appropriation in our vocabulary—but as teenagers we knew that posers were people who pretended to be someone they weren't to look cool or fit in. Anyway, all of these events were somehow well attended. Maybe it was due to the times of the mid- to late nineties. I can't imagine trying to do something like this now and hoping for a quarter of the attendance.

Been to a mall lately? The West Manchester Mall, after spending years as a dead mall, with lots of vacant space, revamped itself into an upscale strip mall. It wouldn't even be possible to hold an evangelistic event in that space today. We also took our puppet show to the nursing home as part of that ministry, although Rebecca and I were always shy when were supposed to visit people in their rooms. We let the adults do most of the talking while we stood around awkwardly waiting for it to be over.

With so much time spent at church and related events, church was our social world, and it became like a family. In more traditional churches like the one I currently pastor, we pass the peace. In my childhood church our greeting time consisted of hugs, handshakes, conversation, and playing with other kids; this version of passing the peace (and we never would have called it that, if we called it anything at all) was a lot longer—and noisier. I learned firm handshakes from the businessmen in the congregation, including Pastor George, who was also a businessman before his conversion. It didn't matter that I was a kid; I got the same handshakes they gave to other men. Of course now I have to remind myself to try not to crush church ladies' hands (I must actually be doing a good job, because a man in his nineties recently told me my handshake should be firmer) because as a kid I learned that the proper handshake should let the other person know that you had a firm grasp and you definitely did not have arthritis or carpal tunnel. Also, there was a fair amount of machismo: you wanted people to know you were a real man, and not some kind of sissy (this was the nineties, obviously not politically correct for our current times, although no one would have cared to be politically correct in our church). It was a different era. I even remember, much to Mom's chagrin, Pastor George quoting in a sermon from the King James Version about King Ahab's ruthless slaughter:

> And it came to pass, when he began to reign, as soon as he sat on his throne, that he slew all the house of Baasha: he left him not one that pisseth against a wall, neither of his kinsfolks, nor of his friends. (1 Kgs 16:11 KJV)[5]

Of course, Rebecca and I thought that was hilarious and had to repeat it several times. "Hey Mom, can we go pisseth on the wall?"

To return to my previous point, we spent a *lot* of time at church, not even exaggerating. Services were very long: two hours would have been a super short service. We sure didn't have any hour-long services like I'm

---

5. Try reading that in a modern translation; it's much less interesting.

used to now; they were more likely to be three, maybe even four if the Spirit was really moving. Any Sunday that we had a carry-in meal we would literally spend the whole day there; we wouldn't go home between services. I especially remember a lot of church picnics when we were at the barn, our last location, before it turned into a house church at the end. When I say it was a barn, I don't want to give you the wrong impression—it was remodeled into a church building, with all the amenities. Of course, when the church first moved in during the summer, it wasn't remodeled yet and we had the doors open during the service to let the breeze in.

I remember one interesting incident during one of these all-day church picnics. Rebecca and I were having trouble getting along with Warren and John, two brothers our age who had some learning disabilities and also ADHD. I don't remember what we were arguing about; no doubt it was something childish. The next thing we knew, the four of us were running at each other, throwing punches. It got broken up quickly, and no one was hurt, but I think people were surprised that these two quiet kids got in a fight. Elder Bob was not impressed. He thought Rebecca and I should have set a better example.

Most of these church picnic days were just good, clean family fun. We even had one day with games and activities, a dunk tank (which I volunteered for, and of course Rebecca just walked up and pressed the button), a sack race, tug of war, carrying an egg on a spoon. Dad actually came to visit that day, not something he did very regularly. I even have pictures of him participating in tug-of-war with the other men. It ended up a draw because the rope broke.

We spent the longest time as a congregation at the farm in the re-modeled barn. It started in a hotel, then moved to an old fire hall (un-fortunately, it didn't have the pole anymore as far as I know). We rented space from another church, which was cool because we did some joint youth events, and their youth group was much larger. (We did a few with them even after we moved, and Rebecca, Rachel, and I even joined their youth group for a while when our church's disbanded when we were the only three youth.) Then we went to the farm and were there until Pastor George's health severely declined at the end of his life. The last of us few remaining met at George and Sally's house.

We had relationships with other churches, more than just the one we rented from. Pastor George was friends with a pastor of a Black Pentecostal church in Baltimore from when he used to do street ministry there before he started the church. We would go have services with them, feed people from the community, and hand out gospel tracts (we had the good ones that were like mini comic books). I even remember someone coming up to us later, on the street, asking if we had any more, and we were all too happy to give him a handful. Of course, passing out tracts was much less fun when you went somewhere for something else, like the time my family went to a Baltimore Orioles game with Amanda, our youth leader, and then Mom and Amanda got bored and decided we should go hand out tracts. I remember I tried to give one to somebody on the party deck (the area with picnic tables behind left field) and he thought I wanted an autograph, and I had to say, no this is a gospel tract, I'm giving them out. He wasn't interested and handed it back; it wasn't until later that I wondered whose autograph I almost got. He was in regular clothes, so if he was a baseball player I didn't know it, although he appeared to be an age where it was more likely he was recently retired if he was a player. I suppose he also could have been a sportscaster or a local celebrity of some other variety.

I suppose those comic book tracts weren't too bad. But I remember one time when we got some tracts that looked like money, I think most of them looked like twenty-dollar bills on the outside. You fold it, so that when someone opens it, the first thing they see in big bold letters is: "DIS-APPOINTED? You won't be if you let Jesus Christ become the Lord of your life." We would leave them in public restrooms, drop them on the floor at the grocery store, put them on restaurant tables (not in place of a tip, but in addition to was fine, I suppose, yet still pretty disappointing), wherever—even at school on days that I felt brave enough to leave one on top of the toilet paper dispenser in the bathroom stall. As a kid, I thought this was pretty funny too. Someone will think they just found twenty dollars and then they'll get the gospel message instead. Sure, I bet these tracts got picked up more than any other kind, but I doubt anyone gave their life to Christ after they were disappointed in picking up fake money that told them to follow Jesus. Would Jesus use such deceptive tactics? I'm sure we made a lot of people angry. But the good thing about gospel tracts, especially with the leave-them-in-public-places method, was that you could give yourself credit for evangelism even though you never talked to anyone. What a great way for a shy, awkward kid to get jewels in his crown for all the souls he helped save. By the way, I wonder if this is something my church made up, because I've never heard it anywhere else. Pastor George said for every soul you helped save you would get a jewel in your heavenly crown. Sure, the apostle Paul talks about a heavenly crown (e.g., 2 Tim 4:8), but where did this idea of jewels for souls come from? In any case, this was good incentive to leave tracts around town. I didn't really do any hard work, but if people read them and got saved, I would get credit for it and have a pretty cool crown. Since I didn't directly share the gospel with anyone, though, I was a little concerned that my crown would just be plain gold without any soul bling—so basic.

Anyway, to wrap up the chapter, there were any number of things that made our church unique. Location for one, though maybe that was not as strange since church planting took off in the early 2000s; I guess we were on the cutting edge. I remember the white plastic stackable chairs and overhead projector with handwritten lyrics. (I would have the job of running it in my youth; oddly enough the projector would remind me if I had neglected to clip my fingernails. I suppose I was at an age where you just start to care about hygiene and appearance. Whenever I noticed my unclipped nails on the projector, I would change the plastic pages extra fast.) We were really free form, like a wild jazz session from a 1920s speakeasy version of a worship service—and why not? We were drunk in the Spirit. I'm not too sure what that means now, but back then it meant that the Holy Spirit took over and we just followed the lead, and so we could act a little wild. I don't remember if we ever had bulletins; I think we might have at one point, but they weren't full of hymn numbers (we didn't have hymnals anyway) and calls to worship. I honestly have no idea what was on those bulletins if we did indeed have them at all. Whenever I was at church early for some reason, such as being a greeter or some other extra duty, I would see the worship team rehearse songs and special music. Even Pastor George sang specials, usually southern gospel. He sang well for someone not musically trained. Later during the service, you would indeed hear these songs, but there was always something extra thrown in: different songs that were inspired by the Spirit or someone who would get up to speak, which was almost always unplanned (more about this in a later chapter).

I could go on and on, really, but there were a lot of reasons why we were out of the mainstream. Even the name of our church was an entire sentence long, designed to grab your attention. (Our logo, too, made for pretty cool T-shirts. It wasn't your basic cross and church name—you wouldn't necessarily know it was a church T-shirt until you read it.) It feels odd to talk about denominations like the Assemblies of God, Church of God, Church of God in Christ, and Four Square Gospel like they're the religious establishment; I'm sure they'd be appalled. But compared to us, these churches more closely resembled standard Protestant churches in the way that they were programmed. You could follow the service on a bulletin. Our church was different; you never knew quite what to expect. Each service was almost completely Spirit led. Worship plans were held loosely. We might just keep singing and praying the whole time if the Spirit so moved, or the sermon might go on for an extra hour or two. (Don't make lunch reservations. Good luck trying to figure out what time the service ends: it's over when the Holy Spirit says so.) I never saw Pastor George use notes that I can recall; he certainly never used a manuscript and would have scoffed at the suggestion had anyone ever dared to make it. He was a natural impromptu speaker, up there in the pulpit with only a Bible. I have no idea how much he planned sermons. When preaching he might say anything, like the example from Kings with piss on the wall. Other minor swear words were occasionally spoken from the pulpit that weren't in the text, "shit" being the worst of them since the other minor swear words can at least be found in the King James. This drove Mom crazy, but she forgave him because of his rough pre-conversion background. And of course, she saw him as a father figure—imperfect, but someone trustworthy and dependable. Rebecca and I were always amused by the colorful language. Pastor George could have easily been a comedian or some kind of entertainer. He was funny, but he was also serious. He would make you laugh one moment, be loud and intense the next, like a Southern Baptist, suddenly yelling for no apparent reason, and speak in tongues with a rapid-fire delivery in the sermon or any time during the services. He would get deep into the characters of the Bible and what were they thinking, humanizing them or sometimes building them up to godlike levels. His own stories from life, as a businessman who was not always operating within the law, were always interesting. I won't go into details, even though these are stories he shared freely from the pulpit. It's enough to say that he had a testimony of being a completely transformed, regenerated sinner saved by grace. I never doubted his sincerity, nor do I now, even as I process all of this.

It was a very personality-driven church. I mean that respectfully, though it has to be said, it was a church started by one leader and it depended on that leader. It wasn't a church planted in a community to be succeeded by new leadership. This is a critique I have of my childhood church as well as seemingly all the churches Mom, and later my stepdad, were drawn to. These are congregations that thrive when the leader thrives and close when they decline. There is one exception to the rule that I know of, which is the congregation my parents attended before their current church. It was started by an African American woman and had always been a racially diverse inner-city church. As she moved towards retirement, she began to hand over more responsibility to the Latino/a ministering couple that had partnered with her. This is the only one of these independent Pentecostal/charismatic congregations my parents attended that has had the longevity to survive beyond the founding leader's ministry. I don't mean to be critical of these churches for their independence, but it seems very few of them had the foresight to prepare leaders to pass the torch to a second generation. You can say what you want about traditional denominations and church boards, but the structure keeps a lasting stability for the perpetuation of a congregation. Of course, I know Pastor George and others would have felt stifled by a church board. Then again, who doesn't? (Speaking from experience, sorry leadership team, love you guys.) Pastor George and those like him intended to hear directly from the Holy Spirit and be the one authority in the style of Moses, to lead and guide the people. It might be all right to have an Aaron, but we all know he's just an assistant. Still, it would have been best to have found a Joshua. But all good things must come to an end. He aspired to be one of God's generals, like the name of the video series Mom borrowed from him once—a video docuseries hosted by Roberts Liardon and adapted from his book, with stories of Smith Wigglesworth, Aimee Semple McPherson, Kathryn Kuhlman, etc.[6] He wanted to be like these independent revivalists, starting small and growing his church into a worldwide ministry. Perhaps at the end Pastor George saw us as seeds to be scattered to take the Spirit of his church to new and different places. An unexpected fulfillment for his vision of a worldwide ministry.

Honestly, though, I think his health declined a lot faster than he thought it would. He had hoped and prayed for a healing for what he called his thorn in the flesh, like the apostle Paul (2 Cor 12:7), which might have been a physical ailment for the apostle, although we don't know for sure. I won't go into medical details as that doesn't feel appropriate and, you know, HIPAA and stuff. He waited for a while before seeking medical treatment. When he finally did, he had a negative reaction to the treatment that affected his memory. A few of us stayed till the end, going to Pastor George and Sally's for house church. He was still able to give a good sermon—perhaps much more subdued than before—but whenever we had fellowship

---

6. Liardon, *God's Generals.*

time, he would ask the same questions a few times in conversation, and we would feel bad and answer them as though it were the first time he had asked. He probably would have been better off resting, but I get the sense that he didn't want to let us down. So, he pressed on, fighting the good fight until the end. I don't think he ever had time to plan how the church would end. I have been avoiding writing this next sentence, but it fully describes this situation. The church lived and died with the pastor, for better or for worse. It was a sad ending to a once vibrant faith community. Even though I'm not sure what to think about this church (the main one from my childhood) or about any of the others, really, and even though I obviously feel a need to process all this, it's unfortunate how it ended. I really think Pastor George was just trying to do what he thought was right; that's all any of us can do. My own theology as an adult is much different from what I grew up with, and at one point I actively tried to be as different from my Pentecostal upbringing as I could. Yet, none of us can change our formation; we may change our own culture and faith as adults, but what we learned in childhood will always be with us to some degree. I don't know how many times in sermons I've called myself a recovering Pentecostal—probably every Pentecost Sunday, or every time preaching from 1 Corinthians chapters 12 through 14,[7] and no doubt other times besides those. I can't escape this part of myself, although I have certainly tried. Best to accept that it was what it was, the good and the bad, the weird and the ordinary mundane (even if there wasn't much of that). To fully know ourselves we must accept our child selves. For me, that means the little boy who spoke in tongues and pretended to be a televangelist, laying hands on Rebecca so she could pretend to fall down. What does that mean for me as I enter middle age, a Brethren pastor and seminary graduate who is more interested in thinking Christianity than feeling Christianity, systematic theology rather than a spontaneous word from the Lord (if I'm being honest, which is the whole point of writing all this)? Many of the stories in this memoir are things I haven't thought about in years, somewhat suppressed memories. I suppose it's therapeutic to get it all down, and maybe there are others reading this who have been in similar churches or have friends and family who were/are and need to ponder the phenomena of the Pentecostal and charismatic movement. Let's consider it all together. I'm not trying to make value judgments. Maybe you are? Or maybe you're part of

---

7. Individually, not all at once. My sermons are twenty-five minutes long at most. I'm not Pentecostal anymore, remember.

a church like this and you want to see why someone would leave the Full Gospel church for traditional religion? Well, let's continue to explore these things. The next chapter gets right into the most mysterious phenomena that I can't begin to explain, but only relate from memory.

Chapter 3: **Angels and Demons**

For our struggle is not against blood and flesh but against the
rulers, against the authorities, against the cosmic powers of
this present darkness, against the spiritual forces of evil in the
heavenly places.

—EPHESIANS 6:12

AT OUR CHURCH, ANGELS and demons were real and present, constantly battling in the spirit realm. Just for clarification, I'm not saying those aren't real
beings as Tillich was quoted in the first chapter, but they certainly fall under
the mystery category. At our Pentecostal church we talked about them a lot.
Indeed, people had stories of seeing and interacting with them, as well as
hearing directly from God through the Holy Spirit or even having visions of
Jesus. These were the sort of things we expected, and if you didn't have any
of these encounters we would have questioned your spirituality. You're obviously not in tune with the Spirit if you never interact with the spirit realm.
Everyone who was someone at our church had stories, testimonies of their
own individual experience. However, this wasn't limited to the individual.
There were moments that included the whole congregation. I specifically
remember two such occasions, one involving angels, and another, demons.
Interestingly, both of these occasions happened at the old fire hall location,
and I don't remember any other instances that are on the same level with
these two. Was this perhaps a high point in our collective spirituality? I was
somewhere in the eight- to ten-year-old range during this time, an impres-
sionable age; I certainly never questioned the validity of such things. They
were as real as the music and the preaching, just the sort of thing you should
expect could happen at church, although infrequently.

The angel incident is a foggy memory, in large part due to the fact that I don't think I had been paying much attention when this event happened. It was during one of those long services where the Holy Spirit was moving, and we just kept the worship going. No one was looking at their watch or thinking about a program to follow. We were just going to keep the music going until the Spirit said otherwise. I don't remember if it was before or after the sermon, or if it was one of those services where the sermon never happened because God wanted us to just keep worshiping. It could have been any of those scenarios. As you might expect, a little kid sometimes gets a little bored of these holy jam sessions. I was a frequent doodler: I drew my own comics, drew Pastor George preaching, Tara singing, Daryl playing guitar, Dre playing drums, or my friends Pete, Rachel, and the other kids who were around. Not very good drawings. Rebecca was the artist of the family; I just drew for something to do, to pass the time. I don't know if I was doodling that day, I only mention it to give you an idea of something I might have done in a long service, and this was definitely one of those. I couldn't tell you how long, I remember it was during the day, probably one of those Sunday mornings that stretches into the afternoon. I suppose it could have even been one of those weeklong revival services; I seem to recall this was a period when we were more likely to have that sort of thing. So, I may or may not have been doodling. I was also a frequent daydreamer as a child. Church and school were the primary locations for optimal daydreaming. I might imagine being a famous baseball player when I grew up; that was one type of daydream. More commonly, though, I made up stories in my head: I might be a pirate, cowboy, settler, soldier in the Revolutionary or Civil War. In the daydream I might be myself, or I might be a historical figure like General Grant or a completely made-up character, like Joey, the first mate on Blackbeard's pirate ship. It was like having a movie in my head. Sometimes, if I didn't have a good daydream going the sermon might inspire one: suddenly I'm King David, Peter, or Paul. Maybe I think about the story as it happened or maybe I think about a side adventure for King David in a battle or Paul on a new missionary journey. I might even insert myself as a character into the story, or become the fictional soldier in David's army, Ben the shepherd who decided to leave home and join Israel's army. I guess I was a pretty imaginative kid. This was before video games (rather, before I had them) and smartphones. Alfred Adler has some ideas about daydreaming that may be pertinent to our discussion. He says,

In daydreams of children and of adults, fantasy takes precisely that concrete direction which is supposed to serve the overcoming of a felt weakness. Disconnected to a certain extent from common sense, daydreams tend in the direction of the goal of superiority. This is easily understood as an attempt to compensate, to maintain the psychological equilibrium, which, however, is never accomplished in this way. The process is somewhat similar to that which the child takes in creating his style of life. Where he feels the difficulty, fantasy helps to give him an illusory view of the enhancement of his self-esteem, usually spurring him on at the same time. Certainly there are plenty of cases, where this latter incident is lacking, where the fantasy, so to speak, is the compensation. Obviously such a situation is to be regarded as antisocial, even though it may be devoid of any activity or of any aggression against the environment.[1]

Anyway, all this to give you an idea of what I might have been doing in the middle or towards the end of a three or four hour service, and why I didn't notice the angels.

So, this is how it happened. The worship team was playing music, and then they weren't playing music, or so I'm told—I didn't actually notice them stop. I wasn't really paying attention. The music was going, but when the music did stop everyone said the angels had sung and we had heard the heavenly choir. I was a kid, and they were adults, so I didn't think anything of it, other than—of course the angels sang to us. Why wouldn't they? The Spirit was moving, and we had tapped into the spirit realm.

Even though I was young, I feel like I had some disappointment that I hadn't really noticed where the music came from and had just assumed the worship team was still singing. I'm sure I didn't comment on my inability to notice the angels, nor did I question the adults. If Mom and Pastor George and everyone else said angels had shown up, then I certainly believed them. I didn't ask whether the worship team really was still playing, or if the guy running the sound system had flipped on a cassette tape. None of those thoughts crossed my childish mind. I wonder now, if we'd had an audible miracle (no one claimed to have actually seen the angels), then wouldn't I have been aware that something different and important was happening? Yet, had no one claimed angels took over the music, I would not have thought anything was out of the ordinary. As I said from the start, I'm taking a hospitable approach to the retelling of these memories, so I'm not

1. Adler, *Individual Psychology*, 218.

leading with doubt. Is it possible that this was the first sign that I wasn't meant to be a Pentecostal? Angels show up and I think to myself, this is really long, when's lunch? To be clear, I have no idea what I was thinking, but it could have been as nonspiritual as thinking about food. I just remember a general sense of surprise: Angels? Really? That's cool, wish I had been more observant for this once-in-a-lifetime event that I spaced out on as though it were any guest musician playing their rendition of "Amazing Grace." (By the way, I haven't a clue what the song was—was it a song? One we would know? Or one only known in heaven? Was it soaking music? Pentecostals know what I mean by that.[2]) I have no idea. If I had been so unaware of this phenomenon, does it shock anyone that I became more interested in traditional Christianity by the time I was in college and wanted to get away from Pentecostals and Charismatics? I would be lying to you if I told you I didn't have my doubts about the validity of this miracle as an adult, but my memory is foggy on this childhood experience. Much more foggy even than the time I "saw" the demon in my bedroom or my psyche, or whatever. I can't discount it without simply saying something along the lines of, "I don't believe angels would take the time out of their busy schedules to sing for our little church." For many of my readers that might be a legit statement. Personally, I don't know why angels would go to the trouble of jamming out with any congregation (what would be the purpose?) but I suppose just because the idea sounds strange or unlikely doesn't mean it's impossible. If there was a purpose, God could allow us to hear the worship from heaven; certainly it would fall under the mystery category. A mass, mystical experience, shared by one hundred people,[3] minus one boy who was preoccupied with other thoughts or distractions (the lost sheep of the ninety-nine?). Yeah, as a child in this environment where miracles were expected, I wouldn't have thought my lack of perception was more trustworthy than the claims of the adults, my spiritual betters. I accepted their interpretation of the event without a doubt, although I seem to be challenging that assumption now. If I had a doubt then, I kept it to myself in the

2. It's what I will describe as the freestyle jazz of Pentecostal worship music. It's not really songs or hymns so much as it's a worship leader singing seemingly spontaneous praises to God. It often includes singing in tongues.

3. My current unscientific estimate of how many people were there—it could have been as low as fifty, though; it was a long time ago, and I was a kid. Do you really expect me to accurately remember the attendance? And yes, one hundred served my rhetorical purpose.

furthest corner of my mind, not to be verbalized or even thought of until much later in life (like now).

Of course, the chapter title promised both angels and demons. Did we all collectively see or hear a demon? No, or at least not quite. It was more of a manifestation, like the demoniac at Gennesaret, although minus the legion.[4] I guess in this instance there was only one demon? It happened during a prayer meeting. I think it was a Wednesday night, unless it was a random weeknight since it was a prayer meeting rather than a regular service (we went to church a lot, remember). I don't even think Pastor George was there, which further leads me to believe it was a random weeknight. Lilly, our intercessory prayer leader, was facilitating the meeting. I would say we made it halfway through, and it had been pretty typical up to that point until Robin walked in. Robin was a middle-aged woman, possibly a biker; she always wore a leather jacket, was a sporadic attender, and seemed thoroughly rough around the edges. While some of our congregation were average church people in suits or dresses, some were like Robin, the kind of person you wouldn't normally expect to see at church. Robin and others like her were always welcome, which is as it should be, I don't care if you're high church Episcopalian or low church Pentecostal. If all are not welcome, then your church is doing it wrong. Pastor George's rough background probably attracted people who thought they would be more welcome at our church than other places. He certainly excelled in hospitality. I wonder now, what would a present-day Pastor George do in our era that is fighting about LGBTQ+ issues. Would he have welcomed people most conservative Christians ostracize? Or would he have told them to get lost, and/or try to cast the devil out of them the moment they walked in the door? We'll never know, because I don't remember that ever being an issue back in that day when most stayed in the closet. I didn't know a single openly LGBTQ person until after I was an adult out of high school (I was out of high school in 2004). It was a much different world then, but I do wonder if they would have been welcomed in the same way as a biker like Robin, or the assorted cast of characters at our church back in the nineties and early 2000s.

Getting back to the narrative about the incident with a demon: Robin walked in halfway through the prayer meeting, and went right to the front, which is not an odd thing to do at our church, where anything goes when the Holy Spirit leads. Lilly probably thought Robin had a prayer request, maybe even a word from the Lord. As you've probably guessed

4. Matt 8:28–34; Mark 5:1–20; Luke 8:26–39.

by now, she had a word, but it wasn't from God. Robin told Lilly that she was sent there tonight by Satan to kill her. I don't remember exactly, but I think her voice was a little distorted, nothing so dramatic as in the *Exorcist* or other horror movies, but still she spoke in a creepy voice that was slightly different from how she normally spoke. I don't know if she was armed; I would assume she probably was, but she never brandished a weapon. Instead of showing any fear, Lilly told everyone to gather around and pray in the Spirit. Everyone gathered around Lilly and prayed, at least all of the adults did. I don't remember Rebecca or me gathering around; if we did, we stayed on the periphery—but we probably didn't at all. Everyone prayed for Robin, and Lilly cast the demon out of her. I actually don't really remember this part. I think maybe one of the youth leaders or Sunday school teachers took the kids out. I don't remember specifically, which contributes to my sense of only having been told about the outcome rather than witnessing the exorcism. The more I think about it as I am processing this in real time as I write, I think this is what happened, which only makes sense when we could have had a shooting or stabbing right then and there. So, I'm sure they did the responsible thing and took us kids outside or at least to another room in the large building (the old fire hall)—probably outside, though, as it would be the most responsible thing to do. This was before cell phones were common; someone still would have had to go back in person to check on the situation.

Some things I am certain of: no one called the police or wanted Robin to be in trouble, because they cared about her and didn't blame her for her actions because she was being controlled by Satan. In fact, I believe Robin came to church at least a few more times after, before no one ever saw her again. (No, I'm not being dramatic, she just stopped going to church or went somewhere else; I don't think she attended any of the other locations we moved to.) I also know that everyone there truly believed that Robin was possessed by a demon and that it had been cast out. What do I think now? I think most of what gets called demons are really mental health issues. Even some of the stories in the Bible are probably of this variety. Yet, it does seem like many of the Bible stories, particularly those in the Gospels, are perhaps a result of all the forces of evil clashing with the purest good in the culmination of the person of Christ. There was certainly a spiritual battle going on during Jesus's ministry, so if ever there was a time for demon possession to be real, that was the time. I'm willing to give the gospel stories the benefit of the doubt and believe that Jesus could really have been casting out demons. It is equally possible that he is healing people of psychological disorders, even though no one had the vocabulary for that back then, other than to call it demons. Can people be possessed by a demon now? I don't know; I would consider in most instances it's a mental health issue such as schizophrenia, multiple personalities, even bipolar. Could Robin have really been possessed? I don't know; I lean towards no, but I try to keep my theology open to the possibility, again with my theology of mystery. (Are you tired of hearing about mystery yet? Too bad, I think if any of this charismatic stuff is real it has to be mystery; there are no other words I have to describe it.) Maybe it is my childhood experiences that keep my theology open. I closed my mind to much of these oddities during my college years, but after a brief total rejection of Pentecostalism, as I moved back towards the theological center, there had to be room for some of these things to at least be possible. I'm still grappling with it all, and sometimes I'm not quite sure what I believe about angels and demons. I don't go looking for them, nor do I expect to see them, but they might be out there. If so, I don't think we're really meant to know it; it's just something going on in another dimension in the background that most people don't take any notice of. Most of us are perfectly happy to keep it that way too. Although faith communities like my childhood church actively seek out the spirit realm, and they find it—whether real or not I don't know, maybe some of both. Yet, I wouldn't say that anyone was putting on an act; everyone seemed sincere. Perhaps I'm the most tempted to consider the time with angels singing to be a hoax compared to anything else. During my skeptical period I probably thought it was, if I thought of it at all. So many of these memories were repressed when I didn't know what do with them—not that I know now other than to put them out there and let others consider them along with me. But now that I'm trying to look at it all objectively, I have to consider all the possibilities. Also, on a personal level, I found Pastor George and other church leaders to be trustworthy and never found any reason to doubt anyone. The church really was a family, where everyone cared for each other. Pastor George and others often helped Mom. I don't think she ever asked, but on occasion she was blessed with money, groceries, or dinner out that was paid for. Now, I know some will be suspicious when they hear about a single mom being given gifts, but there was never anything inappropriate about it. For anyone who knows my mom this is obvious, as she always seems completely Spirit focused to a fault. Unfortunately, there are so many stories of women who are taken advantage of by religious leaders, but this was never something that happened with my mom at our church. I know there were a few single men who were interested, but their interest was never reciprocated. Not that there would have been anything wrong with Mom dating one of the single men; she just didn't care to. None of these men were in leadership, and all of them were very short-term members (attenders—I don't think we really had formal membership). If they were only looking for a single lady to go out with them, they simply moved on to another church.

I remember two of them tried to connect with me and my interest in baseball. One man, Craig, who I think was Japanese, claimed to have pitched for the Seattle Mariners when he was younger. At the time I checked my baseball cards, but I didn't have any of him; this was the early nineties, so I didn't have the internet. Who knows whether he was being honest; I don't think Mom believed him though. I don't remember his last name, so I can't check now. There was later an incident where people from the church went out to Pizza Hut for lunch. Craig went outside to use the ATM; when he came back into the restaurant he claimed to have been robbed. There was some skepticism as to whether he really was robbed, or if he just wanted the church to give him money or pay for his lunch at a minimum (which they probably did). I don't remember if he called the police or if he didn't. If I remember correctly, he claimed to have been threatened that he would be killed if he called the police, because they looked at his address on his driver's license. I'm thinking he probably didn't call the police and that is why no one believed his story. Anyway, I think we threw the baseball around a couple of times, so I liked him, even if no one else did. There was another man who liked Mom and gave me a framed poster, which I still have, of all the MLB team logos. At the time I liked the Chicago White Sox. I don't really know why; I liked Frank Thomas, but I had never been to Chicago (actually still haven't unless you count the airport or Elgin, Illinois). But he didn't quite remember accurately and wrote, "Go Red Sox!" on the back. I didn't care, though. I liked the poster anyway. (By the way, the Baltimore Orioles are my team now. Let's go O's.) Mom wouldn't date until she met my stepdad Curtis much later, after my childhood church had closed. All that to say I don't have any good reason to doubt anyone's intentions. Most abusive religious leaders you hear stories about are the type who would take advantage of a young single mother, but I am confident that nothing like that ever happened. Does that automatically mean everything else was as it seemed? No, because there could be other reasons for faking spiritual phenomena, as I think often happens with televangelists and faith healers. Yet, I don't have any evidence to point to anything being false that came from leadership. To be clear, I think many people came in and gave words from God that they just made up themselves. But as far as Pastor George in particular, I can't think of anything that would cause me to doubt his ethics and moral values. Does that mean every word comes from the Lord? No, because everyone is human and can speak from their own perspective rather than God's. But I think he tried his best, and I have to give him the benefit of the doubt. As a child, he was like a grandfather figure. When I was little, I wore cowboy boots and hats because Pastor George did. This didn't last long in my fashion, probably only as long as it was part of Pete's. Also, there was one time in elementary school when someone thought I was trying to be like Michael Jackson,[5] but I was offended, even though I didn't know who Michael Jackson was. But no, Pastor George was my hero. I even think I still have some books I wrote in first or second grade that have stick figure drawings, and Pastor George is the main character. They weren't about church; they were just made-up stories where he was the protagonist. I dropped the pastor title in these tales; they were just George's adventures.

Anyway, Robin certainly wasn't the only one to have demons cast out of her at our church but was the only one to manifest so dramatically. As you will recall from the first chapter, I was always worried that Pastor George would find a demon to cast out of me. It was not uncommon or unexpected for demons to be cast out of people, whether they were called out at random during the service or in a prayer line, or if someone specifically asked to have it cast out of them. As a kid I never doubted the validity of these exorcisms, although they were always terrifying, even when much less dramatic than the incident with Robin. I would have much preferred the angels, even if I didn't pay attention to them.

As I got into my teenage years, I did start to doubt some of my own experiences, such as the demon sightings and other spiritual beings (except for the worst one with the weird little hooded figure). I never doubted anyone else's experiences or the events that happened in community. I did doubt some of the prophetic words, especially in my teen years and later; I began to think many of the would-be prophets were just attention seekers, especially when it was a visitor who hadn't built up any credibility, and I wasn't sure why I was supposed to care what they had to say. I'll cover this topic more in a later chapter. But with a childlike faith, much of spiritual phenomena is perceived as real and is not questioned; and of course Jesus said we are to

5. Did MJ actually do the cowboy look for a while? I don't remember that.

have childlike faith, for the kingdom of God belongs to children.[6] But when you grow up you start to have your doubts; as you're no longer a child, it becomes harder to believe in everything. A parent can choose a faith community, but it will be up to that child to choose for themselves when they come of age (even a nonchoice is a choice just to remain). We should have an examined faith; it is only the immature who accept everything they are told without verifying it for themselves. Of course, this seems to go against what Jesus says. Yet experience tells us that there is a balance. After all, there are so many faiths, and people choose for themselves. My grandparents chose Pentecostalism for themselves; I believe they were raised Anabaptists of some sort (quite common in South Central Pennsylvania). Ironically, I found my way back there and chose that Anabaptist faith for myself as what makes sense to me, because I can't make much sense of Pentecostalism. But I am grateful for the Christian faith environment that I was immersed in. Would I have become a pastor if I wasn't in church so much, with faith such a big part of my life? Only God knows, but I suspect not. As my call story certainly shows, it wasn't something I was actively looking for. But that's enough foreshadowing of later chapters for the time being.

6. Luke 18:15–17.

Chapter 4: **We're Not a Cult, Are We?**

So then, you are no longer strangers and aliens, but you are fellow citizens with the saints and also members of the household of God, built upon the foundation of the apostles and prophets, with Christ Jesus himself as the cornerstone; in him the whole structure is joined together and grows into a holy temple in the Lord, in whom you also are built together spiritually into a dwelling place for God.

—EPHESIANS 2:19–22

HAVING FRIENDS FROM SCHOOL visit church was always interesting, especially in high school. In junior high and earlier, I don't think I thought much about it (although I didn't have very many friends in my younger years, so maybe it's a moot point). I always just assumed that my church wasn't much different from any other. To be fair my only other experience was with the Assemblies of God, which was my version of high church back then. Sure, I went to a Catholic wedding and funeral, but Catholics weren't real Christians anyway, so they didn't count. (Obviously, that is not my view now, but that's how I was taught to view Catholics; a "generous" attitude towards Catholics that I heard growing up was that a few of them were real Christians, but they were caught up in religion, and once the Holy Spirit really gets ahold of them they'll go to a good Protestant—well, really, Pentecostal or charismatic—church and get out of that dead religion.)

Church was described in two ways: either it was Spirit-filled and on fire for God, where the Spirit was moving and flowing, or it was dead religion, more about tradition, doctrine, and going through the motions—what

Diana Butler Bass calls the "frozen chosen."[1] I had never heard of that term, but it's in line with what Pentecostals thought of more traditional denominations. Of course, I had never experienced any of them except for Uncle Dave's wedding at the Catholic Church and my step grandfather's funeral. Otherwise, I didn't know anything about other churches. I just kind of assumed they were a more toned-down version of what we were. People in traditional churches probably prayed in tongues at home rather than in public. They probably didn't fall down when they got into prayer lines, and maybe when there was a prophetic word it only came from the pastor and not a random person in the congregation. As you can tell from my childish hypothesis, I really had no sense what other churches were doing. No doubt when my friends came to church, at first, they thought it would just be a less formal version of what they were used to. Like, you don't have to make the sign of the cross, recite a creed, or kneel when you take communion (all of which is true, but there was a lot more radically different from what their preconceived notions might have been). I'm speculating, but I don't think they expected what they got. I don't know that I would have used the word Pentecostal or charismatic to describe us when asked about it, and if I did, they wouldn't have known what I meant. I probably told them something like it was just Christian; maybe I said independent, or maybe by high school I was saying it was Independent Assemblies of God, which still wouldn't have had any meaning for them. No matter what, I could not have prepared them for the culture shock, or myself, really, for finding out that the church I took for granted as being what it meant to be church was outside of the norm. But whenever friends stayed over for the weekend, church came as part of the deal, and depending on when they were leaving, they might get it twice. I suppose it says something for my friends that they weren't scared away, because several of them were there a bunch of times. Their religious backgrounds were: none at all, baptized Catholic but otherwise none because that was the last time they were in church, Lutheran, and Episcopal. So, my friends either had no religion, or they were high church and nothing could have prepared them for the lowest church possible. I think all of my high school friends were only present for the barn location, but only after it was already converted into a modern church facility. Still, they had no context for charismatic worship, and they didn't know what speaking in tongues was. I guess my high church friends didn't pay attention to the Scriptures about it or didn't attend on Pentecost

1. Bass, *Christianity for the Rest*, 3.

Sunday. However, I would argue that the event of Pentecost in Acts 2 was not glossolalia, as it was simply a miracle of understanding as each heard in their own language. So, I don't think that was actually speaking in tongues the way Paul describes it in 1 Corinthians. At any rate, if they were at least familiar with Acts 2, they would have had some context for what they were witnessing. The truth of the matter is none of my high school friends were very religious. They got confirmed in the church and then they stopped going, or they went on holidays. None of them go to church now, unless they started since I last talked to them, and I don't know that any of them would still consider themselves Christians. They all became nones. (Not nuns—they were a bunch of dudes.[2])

When Johnny came to visit the first time, he said he wanted to ask Pastor George about the seven deadly sins. I guess it was something he learned about in the Lutheran Church. I wasn't quite sure why he wanted to ask him about that, but I had a vague sense of dread. Maybe I thought Pastor George would think he was trying to be a smart-ass or something. It didn't feel like a question that fit our church; it sounded too traditional. I don't remember what I said in response or if Johnny ever actually asked his question. Johnny was a smart kid who was respectful of adults, at least to their face—he might make fun of them later. I'm pretty sure Johnny never really fully expressed what he thought of my church, but I don't think he enjoyed it very much.

My friend Brian was different, though; he definitely expressed himself after going to my church for the first time. I'm surprised that he ever came back. To back up a little, in ninth grade Johnny, Brian, and I were the "triplets." We all wore glasses, were each just a little chubby at that time, and were into skateboarding and punk rock. Freshman year the three of us were very close; we went on separate paths for our later high school years, yet we remained friends. At times, I was closer to Johnny, at other times I was closer to Brian. Sometimes I was closer to other friends and only hung out with them on occasion. I still consider them both friends. I haven't seen Brian in years, but we are friends on social media. I reconnected with Johnny a few years ago—Jane and I went on a DND campaign with him as our DM.[3] It was over Discord, as he was still in Pennsylvania

2. Burge, *Nones.*

3. DND means Dungeons and Dragons and DM means dungeon master, for those of you who don't speak nerd. And I know, some of my more conservative readers are shaking their heads saying I'm playing the devil's game. Why is it the devil's game? Because we're using our imagination? Because there are dragons that we're fighting? Even though

and we are in Indiana. Then Tim, another high school friend on our campaign who had been Johnny's roommate, moved to Maine. We did have one successful campaign. Then we started a second one. Jane said once was enough for her just to get the experience. But the rest of us were still game. I asked to add my seminary friends Marcus and Emily, which added an extra scheduling complication, and we all got way too busy, and our campaign just stalled out halfway through, which I'm told is quite common for DND. Anyway, back to the more distant past . . .

Brian was the kind of person to speak his mind; he was also the type of teenage boy that liked to draw penises and give you the finger (sometimes slightly disguised like pushing up his glasses with his middle finger). So, of course he was a lot of fun for a quiet church kid. But it only took one church service for both him and Pastor George to make an impression on one another. After the service Brian told me my church was a cult. But I was like, no way, we're not a cult, that's like where people drink Kool-Aid and handle snakes, we don't do that, my mom hates snakes, she would never stand for it, and I haven't even drank Kool-Aid since I was like twelve. But he insisted we were a cult; he said it often after that, although he still came along to church if he was at our house for the weekend. I think Johnny took a middle position whenever we were all together. He didn't call it a cult like Brian did, but he didn't defend it as not being a cult either. He probably just thought we were a bunch of weirdos with good intentions.

Pastor George, as it turns out, told Mom after the service that he saw a demon hovering over Brian. Mom told me later after Brian had gone home. Now, I don't know about Brian having a demon. Sure, he was a character, a rebel, definitely not a Christian—but he wasn't really a bad kid. Yeah, he had a T-shirt that said "bust a nut" with a picture of a cracked walnut (I think) that he wore to school, but I don't think he wore it to church. (Maybe he did; that would have made an impression for sure.) At school he didn't really get in trouble that much. I think he smoked weed once or twice, but he wasn't much into that stuff, and never around me, or Johnny for that

---

both C. S. Lewis and J. R. R. Tolkien wrote about dragons, and most evangelicals revere them—double standard anyone? By the way, last time I checked the 1980s were over, just saying. Perhaps the Netflix show *Stranger Things* has gone a long way to normalize DND; then again, my most conservative readers are going, "You've watched *Stranger Things*? What's wrong with you? That show's about the devil!" (It's not.) I give up; you can't make everyone happy, so why try? Some people have either no imagination or too much when it comes to worrying about what is good or evil. Most things in culture like TV shows are neither in my humble opinion. It's more of a gray area.

matter (that I know of). My thought is that perhaps he was making faces during the services, which is pretty likely. I don't think he would have been flipping the bird, unless it was at me, which he might have done discreetly and only meant for my eyes. So it's possible Pastor George saw something like that. Again, I have a tendency towards doubting people have demons, and sure, I was/am partial to Brian. At the time, though, I had no reason to doubt Pastor George saw what he claimed. It was obvious that Brian wasn't a Christian, so I supposed he could have had a demon. I think this made me a little nervous for a while, because I sure didn't want to see Brian's demon or see it manifest in him. Brian was always welcome, but could he please leave his demon at home? But then every time we hung out it was just a good time—skateboarding, playing guitar (I played bass guitar poorly, while he played guitar quite well and I tried to keep up). Brian also went to one of our annual beach trips during the summer, possibly two. (I'd have to check my old high school photo albums to verify: Brian flipping me off at the beach 2001, Brian flipping me off at the beach 2002. I'm not even exaggerating; that's probably what I wrote on the back for posterity.) Ironically, Johnny never made it to one of the annual beach trips, although I'm sure I invited him. Scheduling issues I suppose were to blame. But Brian was just a fun guy, and probably not too outrageous for a teenage boy when we come right down to it. I just don't think there's a very good case to be made for him being demon possessed, it kind of makes me think of a Suicidal Tendencies song that I will probably regret citing,[4] not because it's a bad song, but because now some of my readers are going to be like, "You listened to what?!" and it will make a pretty good case for Daryl's perspective on my music. But that's the next chapter, so let's not get ahead of ourselves. Also, I should say, let's all use common sense. There is a song on this album I would not currently care to listen to because . . . what were they thinking? Maybe they really were on drugs? It made me pretty uncomfortable listening to them as teenager, which is probably why I haven't re-added it to my collection as an adult like I did with so much of my teenage music that I eventually got rid of post college and then was like, why did I get rid of that? Just because other people would be unimpressed? If you know the album, you know which song I'm talking about; I don't even have to say it. (If you've never listened

4. Suicidal Tendencies, "Institutionalized." In the song he insists that he's not crazy; Brian could probably change it to "I'm not possessed." Ironically, they have a song called "Possessed" too. I think most of this was just tongue-in-cheek, but you'd have to ask them. Don't take my word for it. When they re-recorded their first album it was aptly named *Still Cyco After All These Years*.

40

to ST don't worry about it, just ignore this section, thanks.) As a parent, I'm pretty careful what music I listen to in front of my kid. That doesn't mean I don't occasionally want to go down memory lane with my angsty teenage music. I'm not jamming out to classic ST with my toddler, although there are a few songs of theirs that I could jam out to and it wouldn't be a big deal. Now I feel like I should ask you for a Pepsi.[5]

Anyway, it's hard for a Pentecostal kid with no traditional church experience to explain to nonreligious and high church kids what the Pentecostal church is, and why it's not a cult. Yes, I will defend my childhood church as not a cult. Yes, it was unusual, I know that now, and I would not be at all comfortable in this kind of service now. Nonetheless, it for the most part fell under orthodox Christianity when we take it down to the fundamentals. We didn't recite any creeds, although you could ask us if we believe the words of the Apostle's and Nicene Creed, and the answer would have been yes. (We would have had to take it line by line, because most of us wouldn't have known the words.) At the time I didn't know what to say to Brian. He had forced me to confront the fact that my church was different, and before that I was either unaware or in denial. Now I didn't have that luxury, because Brian made it clear that my church was weird. Before that I would have said, well, sure, we're Jesus Freaks.[6] (There's a contemporary Christian song reference for you this time. See, I'm not a heathen.) We were just full of the Spirit and on fire for God. I went with the church youth group a couple of times to an event called Acquire the Fire,[7] and that well describes what our church was trying to do—to be on fire for God. The Spirit was combustible, and we had it; we were nearly convinced we had tongues of fire on our heads.

There was nothing especially cultlike about us. It wasn't a closed off group; anyone was welcome. There was nothing you had to do to be an insider, just come to church. All were equal. I suppose I said before that if you never experienced the supernatural you might have been considered less spiritual, but that's just my perception, not official policy. Also, there were no inappropriate relationships, no incitation rites, no sacrifices, no communes. We were just unique, a little different than most other churches, but nothing was nefarious. Is it possible that Brian was just trying to get to me

5. Suicidal Tendencies, "Institutionalized."

6. DC Talk, "Jesus Freak."

7. This was an event with contemporary Christian music and preaching geared towards youth. Lee, "Teen Mania."

by calling my church a cult, in the same way that he would have said "you're gay"? (Yes, this is highly inappropriate. It was the early 2000s and homophobic jokes and slurs were popular back then—doesn't make it right or okay.) Yeah, Brian was the kind of friend that you knew liked you the more he insulted you. I usually reciprocated half-heartedly as insults were never a part of my love language. But for teen boys in the early 2000s, insulting and making fun of each other was the way you said to your friend, "I think you're a pretty cool guy, you loser." So, maybe Brian calling my church a cult was in line with the name-calling and flipping the bird; it was a part of his persona, just as much as his "bust a nut" T-shirt that he often wore. Something that he really didn't mean to be taken seriously.

I suppose I had a middle perspective between Brian and Pastor George. I didn't want to think of my church as weird or different, certainly not a cult. And I didn't want to think of my friend as demon possessed, if that's what it means to have a demon hovering over you. Even if it doesn't, I don't want to think of my friend having a demon over his head. (Unless it was the demon of homophobic jokes, which would explain a lot. I expect modern culture has cast it out of him by now, because no one says "gay" anymore in casual humor unless they are a complete homophobe. I would cast that demon out of him myself now.) So, I didn't want either one of them to be right, and ultimately, I don't think either one of them was. My church was unique and so was my friend. I wouldn't tolerate either of them now as they were in the early 2000s, but back then it was all I knew. I spent a lot of time at that church, and I didn't know anything else. Also, back in ninth grade I didn't have a lot of friends, so if my friend made fun of me but didn't mean it and it was all a joke in good fun, then I was still going to be friends with him. Besides, he was genuinely funny when he wanted to be. Later on in high school I would make more friends, and Brian matured and grew up a little. He's a perfectly normal guy now. Last I heard he was selling cars at a dealership; I talked to him about it once when I was considering that line of work, and he's really into bike riding now instead of skateboarding. Everyone grows up eventually, even kids that looked a little rough when they were young. I think he turned out all right.

For a more lighthearted anecdote, I remember a time that Randy was hanging out with me on a weekend that my church was visiting a church in Virginia to have a joint service. I guess Pastor George must have been friends with their pastor, but this is the only time we ever connected with that church; there were other churches that we had more regular connections with. Anyway, Randy was a newer friend towards the end of high school. I think this was the first time he experienced my church, and he was/is still nonreligious. I don't think he had been to church much, period. Randy really didn't know what to expect. But he's a good-natured guy who is usually down for anything. The first thing he noticed and commented on were the accents of the people in Virginia. On the ride home he was imitating the pastor: "Y'all come back again." But the other thing that made an impression on him was when we were asked to catch for the prayer line. I didn't give Randy any kind of warning about what he just got volunteered for, probably due to my past experience with Brian. I just assumed he would figure it out and everything would be fine. I myself had not had good experience with being a catcher. At 5'4" I'm not the ideal size for the job; I might have even been shorter than that when I tried it out as a young teenager, but they soon realized that there were others more suited for catching than me. My talents were better utilized as a parking attendant, greeter, or running the overhead projector. (They tried to recruit me for the sound system but I didn't want to work with Daryl, who was in charge of it. Rebecca tried it out for a while and regretted it.) Anyway, that Sunday the Virginia Pastor asked Randy and me to catch. It didn't go well, at least not for the first guy, because Randy was behind him and didn't know what he was supposed to do. I didn't prep him, nor did I rush to help as I assumed he would figure it out in time. The middle-aged man who fell on the floor looked back at Randy like, "Why didn't you catch me?" I think we caught everyone after that. Randy is six feet tall, so he is the ideal size; he just didn't know what being a catcher meant. You the reader should have an idea of what this means this far through the book: people were going to get slain in the Spirit and fall backwards and we were supposed to "catch" them, guide them gently to the floor. We had a good laugh about the whole thing, and he still remembers the accents and not catching the first guy who fell down as Randy stood by flabbergasted.

For those of you who need a reminder, being slain in the Spirit (what a term—the Spirit slays, as the kids these days say) is when someone has hands laid on them and because of the presence of the Holy Spirit they can't stand, and they fall backwards. They might get up right away, or they might stay on the floor for a while. Maybe even for a long time. My church had blankets that they used to cover people who were on the floor. It was probably mainly for ladies in dresses, out of a sense of modesty, but they covered anyone anyway. They were like small blue velvet throw blankets.

I don't know what to think about my childhood experience with this (along with everything else apparently). I know I talked about it in an earlier chapter. It's hard to really get back into that mindset when I have spent so much time as an adult thinking it was all a game/act or not thinking of it at all. I know I didn't intentionally fall down on purpose when I was slain in the Spirit as a kid. But I also know that I found it to be fun, so I know I didn't resist the Spirit too much, because it was a blast. I didn't fall down so much when I got older, and now I would avoid that situation altogether, but should I fail to avoid it, I very much doubt that I would have the same experience. Maybe it's like being hypnotized: if you're not a willing participant you'll resist it, and it won't happen. My open theology says we should leave room for this to be possible and real. I guess when it comes down to it that applies to all of these things. Could be legit, might not be; could be real for some, could be fake for others. I really don't know. We should be open to the mysteries of God; we're not going to understand everything. At the same time, not every experience is beneficial for everyone. For example, I can enjoy a high liturgical service, but Mom would hate it. Where I see and hear the beauty in the Episcopal or Catholic liturgy, Mom would just see dead religion and wouldn't be open to a move of the Spirit through this kind of corporate prayer and symbols in word and sacrament. Everyone should find what works for them. As it happens that is exactly what I did; that led me to where I am today. We should not fear each other's differences but should embrace them. That is part of what I am trying to do in writing this memoir. It's both an attempt to deconstruct and to affirm, if that makes any sense. It's both/and. I probably sound critical one moment, while I sound like I'm unquestionably accepting the next. I'm processing things I don't understand. I'm doing so with what I hope is a generous spirit, while also calling some things as I see them. I think it's necessary for coming to terms with who I am and who I was back then. It's a journey of self-discovery, and I have invited you to join me along for the ride. Hopefully, everyone will read this with the intention I have of objectively considering a different kind of Christianity. It doesn't suit everyone, but for those who choose it, let's celebrate it for them, even as we examine it and note the flaws, as indeed we all have flaws. There is no perfect Christianity on this side of eternity; we're all just doing our best. I'm willing to extend that good faith to my childhood church and all other Pentecostal and charismatic churches.

I will relate one last story in this chapter, although I was reluctant to because it's only a secondhand anecdote. It's a story of an experience similar to being slain in the Spirit. Lilly shared her testimony, or maybe it was her daughter Amanda who shared it. Either way Lilly at least once—but I think it was twice—had extended moments of being in the Spirit. She was in the Spirit for at least a day; maybe it was longer than that. I remember Amanda said that her parents were selling their house, and she and her dad weren't sure what to do about Lilly, because she was still in the Spirit. I think she was laying on a couch, so they decided to just throw a blanket over her when people were coming over to look at the house. They just hoped she wouldn't giggle or speak in tongues while potential buyers were there. It was kind of a funny story, but also a strange story. I feel like maybe Amanda is the one who told it, because I don't remember Lilly saying anything about what she saw or heard, where she was, etc. Is this like what Paul talks about in 2 Cor 12 as being called up into the third heaven? And what does that even mean? I think Pentecostals might explain such phenomena as something like what happened to Lilly: an out-of-body experience, possibly, or the soul going on a spiritual journey while the body is present on earth but essentially inert (unaware of what is going on around them physically while in the Spirit).

I don't much know what to think of this now (surprise). I know back then I heard the story and thought, wow, Lilly really is a special spiritual lady. I suppose even now I think, well, what would be the point of lying about it? Is it really that wonderful to have a small congregation think you're that special if you aren't? Would it really boost someone's ego to make up a story like that, just so they could laugh and say, those gullible folks at church sure bought my tall tale? For what? Maybe a paid minister might have some incentive to add to their spiritual resume, but an unpaid intercessor? What would she really get out of making up a yarn? Of course, the next thing the skeptic might say is, well, maybe she was having a nervous breakdown. Or maybe she was just stressed and decided to take a break from everyday life and check out. I suppose those are valid hypotheses. But if she had a nervous breakdown, why would she just get up the next day and be back to normal without any kind of psychological intervention? That doesn't seem too likely, and if she just wanted a break from life and decided to fake a spiritual experience, that feels like a lot of work, to not be able to eat, drink, or go to the bathroom, and then to stay in character while potential home-buyers come to look at the house. And no, I don't think she did it to scare them away, because they did sell their house and move to another one that I assume she also liked better than her old one. So, when we consider the other explanations for what happened with Lilly, nothing seems to make more sense than she had a genuine mystical experience. When I find myself skeptical of something charismatic, I look at other places/sources: what have other Christians said about it who are not linked to Pentecostalism? For that I look to Julian of Norwich and her book *Showings*, where she talks about the revelations or showings she received during a period of visions. I also look to Teresa of Avila in her book *Interior Castle*, where she describes her spiritual experiences that also seem to be in the same category. These women mystics seem to be in line with what Paul is speaking of with the third heaven as far as I can tell, which I think is more of a spirit realm than a place you can go to physically. It's a place of the mind, heart, and soul; the body just doesn't have much to do with it. Do I think this is a rare occurrence? Absolutely. But is it possible? The apostle Paul seems to say so, as do Julian and Teresa. Yes, my mind is inclined to skepticism, and if some random person on the street started talking to me about that time back when they were in the third heaven, I would think to myself, this person is definitely crazy—think I'll excuse myself from the conversation quick. But it seems to be the sort of thing that you don't really say much about if it's real. Paul is vague on it; Lilly was vague too. Julian and Teresa seem to share details that will be helpful to their readers while perhaps keeping some of their experiences to themselves at the same time.

Oddly enough, I feel more inclined to be sympathetic to the mystics, perhaps because it so obviously fits into the mystery category that I'm so fond of—it's right there in the name "mystic." It's not meant to be explained. I don't have to feel like less of a Christian because I haven't had such an experience. It's enough to say, wow, I'm really happy for those who do and for what they have shared with us throughout the ages, as in these books. It's like my misunderstanding of the stigmata I discussed in the first chapter. If Francis of Assisi really had that happen to him, it was something special, not something scary, and not something that we should all be trying to attain for ourselves—just something one special holy man experienced that showed just how in tune with Christ he was. If Lilly went to the third heaven, or even if she just needed to be still for a day or two as directed by the Spirit, then I'm happy for her and find no reason to question it. If there was cause to be suspicious or evidence pointing to trickery, I would be the first one to tell you how fake she was, but as there was no reason for dishonesty, I don't see the point. It's not like she was Craig telling a little boy he was a baseball player to impress him so he would help convince his mom to date him. It seems all the nefarious people at my church were those on the periphery, and they didn't stick around long. I think for the most part, Pastor George and the church leadership had nothing but good intentions. I'll critique Deacon Daryl in the next chapter, but even he didn't necessarily have bad intentions. He was wrong anyway—but we're all wrong about lots of things without intending anyone harm.

Chapter 5: **Plain Clothes and Holy Music Only**

Therefore, as God's chosen ones, holy and beloved, clothe yourselves with compassion, kindness, humility, meekness, and patience. Bear with one another and, if anyone has a complaint against another, forgive each other; just as the Lord has forgiven you, so you also must forgive. Above all, clothe yourselves with love, which binds everything together in perfect harmony.

—COLOSSIANS 3:12-14

AS YOU MIGHT HAVE guessed by now, my love for punk rock was going to get me into trouble. Maybe if Rebecca and I had stuck to Christian music only, we would have been all right. But then I got New Found Glory, which might have been okay, followed by Saves the Day's album *Can't Slow Down*, which might have been fine. *Through Being Cool* definitely would not have been. I borrowed it from Johnny once. The cover with the party scene on the front probably made Mom suspicious. She read the lyrics and said give this back to Johnny, this is inappropriate. Indeed, the f-word is in the song "My Sweet Fracture." Then I got Dashboard Confessional. There wasn't any swearing, but the song "Screaming Infidelities" was probably questionable. Then Rebecca and I started telling Mom that the CDs we wanted didn't have any swearing, when in fact we didn't know for sure, and we turned out to be wrong. I even snuck in Rancid's self-titled album, which has loads of swearing, but good luck reading the handwritten lyrics in the booklet—it looks as bad as my handwriting. (Tim Armstrong, you and I need to take a penmanship class together. Once in high school a teacher wrote on my test, "This hurts my eyes." I had a good laugh about that and probably wrote just as sloppy on the next test.) Anyway, I'm pretty sure I kept my Rancid album out of sight due to the skull and crossbones cover art. I suppose I could have lied and said it was a pirate band playing sea shanties with songs about buried treasure and sword fights (that would be kind of like the metal band Alestorm). Easier just to hide it though. Then Rebecca got System of a Down's *Toxicity* and I knew we were in this together, pushing our luck. But if only we had limited ourselves to MxPx, the O.C. Supertones, Stavesacre, and Dogwood,[1] the Christian rock we started with, we might have been all right. We got careless, and we wanted to listen to the music our friends liked, because we liked it too.

I guess Mom started to rightly distrust some of our new secular rock music we were slipping in. Now, I can't remember if Mom asked Deacon Daryl for help, or if he offered his assistance, or if Pastor George suggested it, but one thing led to another, and our music was demanded for inspection. However, we were allowed to hand it over ourselves, so naturally we didn't give them everything. I kept anything with swearing. I wasn't sure about Saves the Day and New Found Glory, so I took out the lyric books and gave them the CD only, figuring if they heard some nonthreatening pop punk with no swear words I'd get it right back. I also took out all the heavy metal, even though it was Christian—Zao, Blindside, Living Sacrifice. I figured if they popped one of those into the CD player, they'd pop it back out in a hurry and then cast the devil out of me. So, those got held back too. Everything else I put in a big cardboard box in good faith that it would be coming right back to me, maybe even with an apology for doubting my choices. Obviously, this was a disingenuous attitude and a bit arrogant—but I was a teenager, so . . . Also, Rebecca did the same—we probably discussed it and made a plan—although there was one thing we did different from each other. I initially gave my sketchy music collection to Brian, while Rebecca

---

1. Funny tangential story that's hopefully worthy of a footnote: freshman year I had a Dogwood T-shirt, plain black with just the band name on it. One upperclassman, I think a senior, saw my T-shirt and thought it was a euphemism. Obviously it's not, as Dogwood is a very Christian band. I'm sure they're named for the tree or the flower. Anyway, he thought their name was a euphemism, but he would forget what the name was and mix them up with The Squirrel Nut Zippers because in our original conversation at the beginning of the school year he said, "That's like that band Squirrel Nuts!" and I was like, "Uh, sure it is, whatever you say buddy," and so he would always call me Squirrel Nuts any time we would pass in the hall. I don't think I ever corrected him, just found it amusing. I don't think either one of us knew each other's name. If I knew his I've long since forgotten; he was just that weird guy who always called me Squirrel Nuts.

hid hers in her backpack. Eventually, I switched to Johnny as my music holder—I think partly because he lived closer, so I had easier access, and I think I just perceived him as more trustworthy. That and I knew he wouldn't get annoyed about it, whereas Brian would probably at least have comments and make fun of me for being in the situation in the first place. My solution turned out to be the better choice as Rebecca's CDs were found, her collection was mostly nu metal at that time. Besides System of a Down, she had Staind, Linkin Park, Seether, and Disturbed. She also had some Christian metal: Project 86, P.O.D., Anguish Unsaid, Prosper, and Like David. After she was caught, she realized that my method was better.

At first, we didn't really do anything other than wait, because we thought our music was coming right back sans Rebecca's seized backpack contraband, which no doubt ended up in Daryl's trash can. But the process dragged on. What were they doing, writing a thesis on Christian rock? Being music enthusiasts, we weren't going to not listen to music, so we got what we had back from Johnny and burned copies; that way if they were found we didn't really lose anything, as the originals were safe back in Johnny's care. We did get caught with burned CDs at least once, but it was relatively painless as we just burned them again according to plan.

As the days turned into weeks, dragging on and on, Rebecca and I talked about going to Daryl's house when he was on vacation to break in and take our CDs back. It wouldn't be stealing because they were ours anyway. Rachel said she would help, but I don't know how serious we were. Maybe we had flashbacks to the time we went to Rachel's youth leader's house (she was briefly at another church) when they weren't home. We were going to get beef jerky for a youth fundraiser. When we found they weren't home Rachel said, "Let's go to the back door, they always keep it unlocked." Rebecca and I said, "Well, don't you think they would probably not want us to do that?" To which Rachel replied, "We're getting it for the fundraiser to sell for the church, why would they care? Besides, if they care so much why don't they lock their door?" So, we said, "Well, it's your youth leader, you probably know better than we do, so okay, let's go get that jerky." As you might imagine they were unimpressed by this logic when they found out, and I doubt our mediocre sales really did much to smooth things over. Perhaps Rachel's being ready and willing to break into Daryl's house made us realize just how bad of an idea this was, so we never did it. Although when he came back from vacation, we were still kind of wishing we weren't so responsible. After a few months Mom shared with us the findings of their investigation. Some of the CDs had questionable artwork, supposedly there were pictures of demons hidden in the designs. (Pillar's *Above*, which has very religious lyrics—I'm sure if there were demons in the picture they were probably cowering in the corner or being defeated by a heavenly being. I never confirmed it one way or the other as I had moved on from rap rock by this point anyway. They might have been completely full of it for all I know.) Or, in another example of cover art critique, what they said looked like scratch marks over a picture (!?), intended to be artsy I'm sure, was really violent in their eyes. (Looking at you Element 101: apparently *Stereo Girl* is secretly very angry music. Did they even listen to it?) Also, when Daryl put on some of our CDs, he said the way his toddler danced to the music didn't seem normal, so it must be devil music as he suspected all along—seems an absurd way to judge music as evil, based on toddler dance moves. Now, keep in mind that ninety-nine percent of this was Christian music with a couple of harmless secular ones thrown in for credibility. It was decided that our music would not be returned. Daryl burnt us a copy of a worship CD he had that contained two rock songs on it; the rest of the songs were church music through and through. We weren't too interested in his CD. I think we both listened to it once, and our reaction was, meh. Eventually, at least another month later, our CD collections were sold by Daryl, and we were given the money.

We even lost our homemade music videos, which were also confiscated and I assume thrown away, videos where we sang along to our music. We had a "band" with Rachel and sometimes Johnny, where we simply sang along with our favorite songs, although Johnny usually opted to lip synch rather than sing. The first video we made Amanda filmed for us, and we called ourselves Pray for Us to Sing Better or PFUTSB, properly pronounced PeeFutzBee. It was a play on the contemporary Christian band Pray for Rain or PFR. We didn't take ourselves seriously; it was just for fun. But these videos were thrown away. Thankfully, we still had most of them on the little video camera tapes (I know I'm talking about old timey technology again, sorry kids) or friends had a copy of the VHS that we were able to copy. The only one we lost was PFUTSB 2, which, ironically, was only Christian music except for "Ten Minutes" by the Get Up Kids, which I sang, and "My Name is Jonas" by Weezer and "My Girlfriend's Shower Sucks" by Goldfinger, which Johnny lip synched. All completely innocuous songs. These were purely innocent kid music videos where we even tried to imitate the silly filler content between songs that we saw in the old *Tooth & Nail Records Video Compilation* that Rebecca and I had on VHS (also taken away with everything else).

Well, Mom didn't know that we held back all of the music that she could rightly disapprove of. Our music collections were once eighty percent Christian or more; now that number was flipped and our music was mostly secular. We still liked Christian rock, but our music collections were heavily secular for a long time after that before we added more Christian music to balance it out. So, it seems the purge of our music had the opposite of the intended effect. We continued to add to our collection and have Johnny hold them for safekeeping. It worked almost too easily; we wouldn't hold the originals any longer than it took to burn copies. We were never caught with the originals other than Rebecca's initial backpack contraband, and when our burned copies were found we would say Johnny gave them to us, which was technically true. Oddly enough, around this time Christian emo took off. While I was jamming with Rancid and Bad Religion, Brian was getting down with the likes of Further Seems Forever and Mae. While I always liked Further Seems Forever, I never much got into the emo scene. By emo I mean the early post-punk mellow/emotional rock jams, not the caricature of semi-goth popular screamo that everyone eventually came to associate with emo. This was a *peripeteia* (fancy literary term meaning ironic reversal). I never managed to get Brian interested in my Christian punk rock, but he loved the early emo, while I wasn't too interested and wanted the most cathartic punk rock I could find, even NOFX. (Don't look that up if you're super conservative, please and thank you!)

I'm not proud of all this youthful deception, pretending to cooperate while in actuality we were rebelling to the max (which I guess is very punk rock at least). Rebecca and I never told Mom about it, so if she's reading this now, she knows. I guess we were two angry kids,[2] like the Street Dogs song. (Rebecca and I always kind of identified with this Street Dogs song in our college days, although most of the lyrics besides the chorus don't actually sound too much like us). I would guess it's probably not a shock for Mom reading this now, and she might have suspected something like this was going on in the shadows; we might not have been quite as clever as we thought we were, only just clever enough not to get caught holding the goods. Later on, when I was in college, Mom accidently knocked over my CD rack and when she tried to put it all back, she couldn't get Gogol Bordello's *Gypsy Punks: Underdog World Strike* back in the slot, so she looked at the back

2. Street Dogs, "Two Angry Kids."

cover and saw one of the songs had the f-word in the title. So, I had to take my CD collection and put it in the trunk of my car until I got an apartment a year or two later. Had she looked at Rebecca's music she would have found the same stuff—I think even that very same Gogol Bordello album—but Rebecca didn't have a top-heavy CD rack that toppled over, so she didn't get caught. I guess we had a reversal of luck this time around: now I was the one with illicit contraband. I even remember one time carrying around a duffle bag or two with Johnny because my car was getting worked on and I didn't want my entire music collection to be vulnerable to theft; no doubt the garage was full of punk rockers who would have thought they hit the jackpot. So, we each carried a heavy duffle bag around a park and the mall, killing time until my car was fixed. Johnny really was a good friend to always put up with my nonsense that I doubt he understood at all, since he was allowed to do pretty much whatever he wanted. I doubt his parents ever questioned or even cared about what he had in his CD player. He was the definition free-range child and grew up just fine.

Back up a little to senior year when I was almost eighteen: I started feeling a little guilty. By this point I had gotten approval to listen to Five Iron Frenzy and Poor Old Lu. I decided in September at the beginning of the school year to only listen to those two albums, just the music I was allowed to listen to until my birthday in October. Thankfully, Poor Old Lu was a double album, *Mindsize* and *Sin*. But still, listening to the same three albums for a month and a half got pretty old. The Five Iron Frenzy album was *Five Iron Frenzy 2: Electric Boogaloo*. I still like and occasionally listen to those albums, but I probably waited until I was at least nineteen to listen to them again after my eighteenth birthday. They were pretty well seared into my brain; I probably could have sung them a cappella from start to finish in the correct song order with no mistakes. I can't do that now, but back then I could have, I'm sure. By the way, those who know me well and have ridden in the car with me know that I have a variety of music. I don't care for repetition. When I get new music, I try not to have it on repeat, so I don't get bored of it. I try to mix in enough of the old music to keep the new music fresh longer. Also, for anyone who goes to my church, you have not heard my music, and that is entirely on purpose. Not because I'm ashamed of it, but because I know you would much rather hear some Mozart, Beethoven, Brahms, or something sophisticated like that, so I keep my noise to myself and we either ride with conversation or some nice NPR; it's a professional courtesy. Yes, I know, I should listen to some nice contemporary Christian music; I tried, it didn't work. I just can't get into it, even though as a pastor I'm supposed to like it. But in that same period that I force-fed myself contemporary Christian, I also started listening to Skillet; I actually got Jane into them, and I think she actually likes them even more than I do. Jane does listen to contemporary Christian music, which is fine, but she likes some of my noisy music too.

Well, this chapter is about more than music; perhaps if Daryl had stopped there, we would have been cool. We might have said, well, he took away our music, but he is a deacon, so we should respect him and forgive him for the error of his ways. But Daryl was just getting started. He decided we needed help to become good Christian kids rather than a couple of hooligans. He would stop by our house, at least weekly, to make sure our chores were being done. I remember one time there was a pencil that was left out on the table, and he made a big deal out of it, and we were just like, it's one pencil, dude, get over it. The whole house isn't a mess just because there's one lonely pencil on the table that should be in the pen and pencil cup. But to him, we were disrespecting our mom and being slobs. Back then I worked at McDonalds; one day I came home from work early, and I thought I saw his car, so I turned around and drove to the mall or something and came back later only to find out that I had missed a visit from Grandpa, who had a similar car to Daryl's. We dreaded visits from Daryl. It was worse for Rebecca because she was too young to work or drive; sometimes I got lucky and missed him due to work and his spot-checks being at random. It was a lot of stress for teenagers who had other things to deal with and couldn't even de-stress with our jams (well, not openly anyway, as we've established).

The other weird thing we couldn't figure out was the sudden rule that we could only wear plain clothes, no logos. I suppose Naomi Klein would approve.[3] Granted, we had a lot of band T-shirts, so it would have made sense if those were removed. I had a lot of skate T-shirts too, but they were all tasteful; certainly there are plenty of inappropriate ones I could have had, but I never tried to get away with anything like that. I guess one could say skateboarding is kind of sketchy, but I was still allowed to skate, so that didn't make sense. I think I had at least one Adidas shirt, maybe even an old Nike shirt in the bottom of my drawer that I had stopped wearing for being too jock, but that was out too—literally everything, any kind of graphic, was banned. The only thing I got away with was a Volcom polo

3. Klein, *No Logo.*

shirt that had the logo embedded within a stripe. Thankfully, Daryl the fashion cop laid down this edict at the beginning of the school year, so we were allotted a clothing budget. Rebecca and I both balked at the idea of wearing plain T-shirts; we associated them with "treads." Yes, I know you have no idea what I'm talking about because I think "tread" is a word exclusive to Red Lion, Pennsylvania, and I don't even know if it is still in the vernacular. I suspect not, but people from Red Lion my age know what I'm talking about. Tread means the same thing as redneck; we had so many of them that we coined our own term—way to go Red Lion for being linguistically interesting. Anyway, treads wore plain T-shirts. I was not a tread, therefore I didn't wear T-shirts that year. I spent an entire school year wearing polo and plaid shirts. I even had a few Hawaiian shirts, but I didn't wear them often; they were a little too cheerful for my angsty teenage persona. The preps (is that still a word for the fancy rich kids at school?) probably thought I was trying to become one of them, although our mutual ignoring of one another probably told them otherwise. Maybe the girls thought I was trying to make an impression. If that was a side motive it wasn't as effective as talking to them would have been, but what can you do when you're shy and have no self-confidence? And dealing with an overbearing deacon probably didn't do anything to help.

Sometime later Mom told us that Daryl's strict rules were a result of his time when he was in a reformatory boot camp as a troubled youth. He was imposing things on us as mouthy, sloppy, slightly rebellious teenagers that were imposed on him for doing drugs and more serious offenses. Why were we being treated so harshly for typical teenage behaviors? If we needed anything cracked down on us it should have been with our schoolwork, which was horrible, mine in particular; but I don't think Daryl ever inquired about it, and I think Mom felt bad enough about our private boot camp not to suggest anything else he might want to check up on us for. Mom eventually put a stop to the whole thing, and we went back to normal, or normal but still sans music. We could get the clothes we wanted again, except no band shirts at this point—I got them again when I was eighteen and I think Rebecca did too. But otherwise, we could leave our pencils out on the table and wear clothes that Naomi Klein disapproves of. (Sorry, not picking on her. I think she has valid points, just not ones that teenagers would care about.) Ironically, the only band T-shirt I currently own is an old Beatles T-shirt; I feel like most of the music I listen to no one else knows, so what's the point in wearing band shirts? Although I literally saw a man my age wearing a Rancid "Outcome the Wolves" T-shirt that I used to own in high school or college, I forget which. It's just funny that now that I can, I choose not to. I also never got a mohawk, because by the time I moved out of the house I was too mature and professional to want one. I would have totally rocked it in high school though and had fun, but whatever. I got away with some long spikey hair like Guy Fieri (of *Diners, Drive-Ins and Dives*) for most of my high school years, but the last time I spiked my hair was the beginning of senior year. That brief period included when I sat for my senior picture. In the portrait I have spiked hair and a suit and tie; it's actually not a bad picture of me either. Oh well, more people probably would have thought I was a weirdo if I had the mohawk, so maybe it was for the best. There were probably enough people who thought I was an oddball as it was without taking it to the next level.

I bet some of my readers are wondering what this chapter has to do with Pentecostalism. Well, for one thing this is also a coming-of-age story, so this chapter falls entirely under that genre. Also, it does indeed have to do with Pentecostalism, because it was the church environment that made the situation possible. At most churches the deacons don't have much power; my church now doesn't even have deacons. The previous Brethren church I attended had two nice elderly ladies as deacons and they helped serve Communion. I don't think their deaconly duties went much beyond that. I can't imagine either of them doing a quarter of the things Daryl did. Honestly, they just serve Communion, and otherwise one forgets that they're deacons; if I wrote a book about them, they would not have the word "deacon" permanently affixed to their name like Deacon Daryl. It would be a complete afterthought, if it was even noteworthy enough to be mentioned at all. I'm sure if someone ever thought of consulting them about an unruly youth, which isn't likely, they would either refer someone to the pastor or suggest counseling. But in my childhood congregation, deacons and elders had a lot of power and responsibility. They were almost as important as the pastor, and you sure didn't want to get on their bad side. The consequences were unpleasant. As a part-time pastor of a small church, I wouldn't mind having some deacons and elders to share the workload (by the way, these people were unpaid volunteers); I would be happy to have someone to delegate tasks to! Even so, I wouldn't suggest anyone try to create their own youth boot camp or even do something intrusive like go through their kids' music, even if their kids are listening to some very inappropriate music. Rules on music and other media should be between the parent and child;

having an overzealous middleman won't do you any favors. Also, kids come to a certain age where they need to make those decisions for themselves; authoritarian rule only causes kids to hide things, and you lose all chance of having any influence. A better approach would be one that is friendly and open, offering advice but not dictates. It's different for young children, but teenagers need to start getting some autonomy, as you're preparing them for adulthood. You shouldn't want them dependent on you for every little thing. You give them the tools to make good choices and then you let them have the freedom to make mistakes, and they will. But they learn more this way, and you will retain your status as a trustworthy guide and giver of advice. Take it from someone who decided they would be their own guide, their own voice of wisdom. It doesn't work out well. I sometimes wish I had more positive relationships with adults as a teenager; I think I could have benefited by having more mature people to ask questions. I don't blame Mom for this; it's hard being a single mother, and when help is offered it makes sense to take it—but from someone who isn't helpful the "help" does more harm than good. I think Daryl is someone who had a hard life and didn't really know how to interact with people. He later had problems with his family relationships and the last I heard was a very unhappy person. I wish someone would have recognized his authoritarianism wasn't good, Christian, strict morals, but rather a grasping for power and control unhealthy in a parent, husband, and church leader, which proved detrimental to his relationships. If all you want to do is control people, eventually, you'll end up sad and alone. I think he needed or still needs inner healing, therapy, prayer, and to do the work to become a whole person. Churches sometimes attract unhealthy people who are looking for power.[4] A small independent congregation with minimal oversight is the perfect place for someone like Daryl to slip through. Really it was a shame. When I was young Daryl seemed cool: he played guitar at church and had the "Jesus look," so guess who got that part during Bible plays. When his wife, Fran, babysat Rebecca and me one summer, we thought she was the strict one and he was nice. Of course, he wasn't the babysitter; he was usually at work, and she handled the discipline just fine herself. I don't remember if that included spankings. She didn't need to anyway; the packets on good manners she created and assigned us to fill out were much worse than a spanking would have been. I guess Fran was no picnic either. All the same, we felt bad for her when we

---

4. DeGroat, *When Narcissism*.

heard about what happened with her and Daryl after they moved out of state and no longer had the mentoring of Pastor George.

It's great when the church has a lot of influence on our lives. However, when that influence is abused, it can have harmful, lasting effects. To be fair, I don't think Pastor George or Elder Bob realized what a control freak Daryl was, and maybe he hadn't always been that way. Maybe he became a deacon before he was truly ready to wield power. It's like when your coworker suddenly gets a promotion and now, instead of being that cool guy you chat with, they become that power junky who realizes that they like holding authority, and they become insufferable. This can happen in any setting—church, work, school, probably the military. (But I wouldn't know about that last one as a good pacifist. Just seems a likely place for it.) I guess this is a caution to those of us who are pastors to be careful who you let in leadership. These days we usually just need warm bodies to fill all the spots; nevertheless, if we see red flags we might want to point those out before we approve someone to be in authority. Of course, in my denomination that's all on the leadership team; I don't really have anything to do with who does what. It's a lot different in a denomination that is much more congregationally run, versus an independent church that was begun by a pastor, and the buck stops with the pastor—total authority. Personally, I wouldn't want that responsibility. There's not necessarily anything wrong with this kind of setup, but I would recommend independent pastors to establish accountability so that they aren't tempted to become an authoritarian ruler or abuse their power in any other way. In my case, it was a deacon, not the pastor, that was a problem. It could just as easily have been the pastor that was a dictator, which could create all kinds of problems. There are plenty of stories from congregations that suffered a full variety of abuses from their pastor. The media is quick to let us know when the big-name megachurch pastors fall from grace.

I have to admit that I like denominations to have much more structure. I don't feel a need for a bishop or anything that formal, but having some guidelines and people to help you along the way is beneficial. I might sometimes feel more like an employee of the church than a leader, but at the end of the day I prefer it that way. The decisions that are made are made collectively; Walter Rauschenbusch would approve.[5] Everything is done communally. There is no individual laying down the law; we're all in it together. Decisions are often made that I personally wouldn't have made or would

5. Rauschenbusch, *Christianity and the Social*, 314–22.

have made somewhat differently, but at the end of the day we all accept the fact that we put our heads together and came up with the best options as we saw fit. Pastor George wouldn't have cared for this style of leadership, and Daryl would have been like, "Really, being a deacon just means I serve Communion? That's kind of a letdown." But it's what works for us. Being independent is what worked for Pastor George, at least when the congregation was thriving. The problem was he didn't have any real network to fall back on and, as I said before, anyone to pass the church on to. I would certainly caution pastors for wanting to be too independent. You don't have to be as communal as my church is, but at least find a happy medium. By the way, lest you think my Brethren church is strange, I'll tell you, I have found that most denominations are the same—it's the congregation that is really running the show. They're the ones that will still be here when we pastors are gone. Yes, I almost guarantee you that if you're in a traditional congregation, your board or leadership team runs the show. The pastor is just a figurehead, the King or Queen of England as it were: we dress up fancy and say important stuff, but we don't run anything. I feel like some pastors might be mad at me for letting you in on that little secret but believe me, it's true, and you're probably better off for it whatever you might think.

Daryl was really the one most responsible for making our lives miserable for that difficult school year, which is a pretty big deal to teenagers who have enough going on with just being teenagers. Our fights about music were really just with him, although I doubt Pastor George would have cared for our music. Yet it all started with Pete skanking[6] to B.O.B., aka Bunch of Believers, in front of the church, and Rebecca and I were like, "Yes! This is what music is meant to be like" and went from there. Christian Ska was our gateway to all varieties of rock music. Yet all through middle school we stuck religiously with Christian rock to exclusion of all else. But maybe that wasn't as safe as we thought, at least as far as Pastor George was concerned. He told one story, I think from the pulpit, about how when he heard one of

---

6. Skanking? The kids are asking, what's that? It's a dance you do to ska music with your arms and legs, basically you kick your legs and swing your arms cross body. There are some variations on it. I mean it in the most respectful way when I say that it almost looks like a Jewish dance with the leg kicks. "But wait, what's ska?" the same kids are asking. Basically, a combination of reggae and punk rock with some other influences such as jazz and swing. I recently heard Amber Ruffin call it "discount reggae" on an episode of the comedy show, *Have I Got News for You* (Wood, *Have I Got News*). I disagree because it's reggae plus other genres, and yes, I still listen to ska. Yes, it's super nineties and I don't care. Just another reminder for you that I'm old now.

Pete's Christian rock CDs[7] he saw demons dancing, so he threw his grand-son's CD in the trash. No wonder Pete eventually just started listening to pop music! He didn't want to have the same kind of fight that we did. Or maybe his tastes just changed; I never asked.

The only music incident I can think of involving us and Pastor George directly was the time Rebecca and I played our guitars in front of the church for the second time. Rebecca played guitar and I played bass. We had played one other time along with our music teacher who played keyboard. Sadly, he passed away during the hymn as we were playing. At least he went out doing something he loved, but it was probably a little traumatic for us—al-though we never would have said so. Rebecca and I didn't have lessons after that, so we mostly just goofed around. Rebecca made her own composi-tions, and I got bass tabs off the internet. The song I could play best was "No Cigar" by Millencolin. Anyway, we didn't have lessons anymore, but we still wanted to play for the church. I don't remember if we were recruited or if we volunteered. But we took one of Rebecca's original guitar instrumentals, all of which were mellow and soothing, and I made up the bass parts for it. It probably wasn't anything spectacular, at least not on my end—Rebecca put a lot more effort into it than I did. But it was hardly Ozzy Osborne, more like a simplified Snow Patrol. After our performance Pastor George commented in front of the whole church that our song was entertainment, not worship, and didn't belong in a church service. We never played for the church ever again after that. I think many people were sympathetic to us, though, probably thinking, they're just kids, and at least they tried to do something nice. I think we mostly just shook it off and thought, well, he's older and doesn't care for our style of music. At least he didn't try to cast the spirit of rock 'n' roll out of us, so I guess it was all good.

---

7. He didn't say what band, and I probably never asked in case I listened to them too.

Chapter 6: **Please Don't Leave Me Behind**

Then two will be in the field; one will be taken, and one will be left. Two women will be grinding meal together; one will be taken, and one will be left. Keep awake, therefore, for you do not know on what day your Lord is coming. But understand this: if the owner of the house had known in what part of the night the thief was coming, he would have stayed awake and would not have let his house be broken into. Therefore you also must be ready, for the Son of Man is coming at an hour you do not expect.

—MATTHEW 24:40–44

BACK IN THE LATE nineties and early 2000s, the most popular Christian novels were the Left Behind series by Tim LaHay and Jerry B. Jenkins. They were so popular that I knew of several people who were not Christian who read the series. They were action-packed thrillers set during the apocalypse. For whatever reason, dystopian literature is popular; even I enjoy it. Although now I would prefer *Brave New World* by Aldous Huxley, *Fahrenheit 451* by Ray Bradbury, and *1984* by George Orwell, to name a few. However, those are novels from my college days; my dystopian literature of junior and senior high was *Left Behind*, and because of its popularity, I didn't feel awkward carrying it around school the way I would have felt about carrying a Bible or wearing a Christian T-shirt (not something I did after elementary school). I think in high school, my embarrassment around my religion got tied up in how my friends responded to my church, so I took all religion as something to be private and keep to yourself (except for the occasional, anonymous, tract drop). But *Left Behind* was cool, and if you asked me about it, I would have given you a vague description like, it's a story about the end of the world and a group of people who find ways to survive while challenging an evil regime. That's not an inaccurate description of the basic plot, but it leaves out the religious aspects of the story. But I figured that wouldn't matter too much because if they were non-Christian they would read the books for the reasons I described, not for the prophetic end-times theology of the novels. Then maybe I'd score some soul brownie points if they came to Jesus through it.

There were also movies. *Left Behind* eventually became a movie series. Before that there was the old classic *A Thief in the Night*, which got the rapture movie genre started. Also, John Hagee's ministry put out two rapture movies, and there were several others that I thought he made, but maybe he just promoted them on his show; some of them had surprisingly well-known actors such as Mr. T and Howie Mandel. Some of these movies I actually got my friends to watch when they were at my house. I don't remember if I was trying to quietly evangelize, or if I just thought they should like it because they were action movies. I suspect my reasoning was a little bit of both. I don't remember them being too impressed. Although Randy actually liked *Bells of Innocence*, which isn't a rapture movie—it's more like a Christian horror movie with Chuck Norris as a cigar-smoking angel (no I'm not making this up), and his son Mike Norris stars as the film's main protagonist. It wasn't terrible for a Christian movie (yes, I expect you don't believe me, and maybe I'm just comparing it to Christian movies that are much worse, but at least it was entertaining). We got the DVD during Mom's *Walker Texas Ranger* obsession; it's safe to say she had a crush. (Hope I'm not embarrassing you, Mom. I think a Chuck Norris crush for women of your generation is probably not uncommon. Besides, you remember all the Chuck Norris jokes about how superhuman he is that were popular during this time, such as in Ian Spector's *The Truth About Chuck Norris: 400 Facts About the World's Greatest Human.*)

Of course, by the time I was in high school, or maybe a little before, I was allowed to watch regular PG-13 movies, and occasionally R, depending on the reasons for the rating. With all the angst over music it's surprising that movies didn't get the same treatment. Maybe that was because Pastor George didn't seem to mind movies either and would sometimes talk about them in sermons. I especially remember him referencing *Simon Birch*, which is actually only rated PG but did have a few moments, if I remember correctly, that took it up to the line where it almost could have been PG-13. Also, I went to see *Twister* in the theater with the youth group when I was still quite young; it was PG-13, and I was younger than 13. So, even though music was a big deal, movies weren't for some reason. Compare that to the brief period Jane and I lived in Mississippi when we were working as house parents in a group home. We would go to the movies fairly often when we were off duty, and it wasn't uncommon to see a group from a very conservative church protesting at the movie theater. That was a moment of culture shock, and there was plenty of culture shock when we lived in Mississippi. Like really, Christians are still protesting the evils of Hollywood in 2016? They weren't protesting specific movies either; they were protesting Hollywood in general. Anyway, at our little Pentecostal church in Pennsylvania during the late nineties and early 2000s, movies were just fine (within reason of course). That probably surprises some of you, but I guess when your church is completely independent it's up to the pastor what to preach against and what to consider permissible. Prior to high school, though, we did mostly watch Christian and family movies that I think were still Christian produced, like *The Buttercream Gang*. (There's a classic; it got a little weird in the second movie, *Secret of Treasure Mountain*, when Eldon Flowers becomes the Christian kid version of Indiana Jones. Maybe you should stay in your lane, Buttercream Gang, but as little kids we were nevertheless entertained, and at least there wasn't anyone eating monkey brains or ripping hearts out. Yeah, thanks for a few nightmares, *Indiana Jones and the Temple of Doom*.) Anyway, when rapture movies became popular, they were in our family DVD collection. Well actually VHS originally. (Don't make fun of me because I'm old. I had cassette tapes too. Last night in conversation, as I was writing this at Church of the Brethren Annual Conference, I heard the term geriatric millennial. So being 40 makes us geriatric now, really?)

Besides in the books and movies, the rapture and the end times were a big deal. I wouldn't say we were obsessed with it the way some evangelicals/fundamentalists are, but it was a fairly common topic for sermons or discussion. It was definitely something we thought about from time to time. As I said before, I was a daydreamer in church (and other places); sermons about the rapture sent my brain on a long rabbit trail as my mind wandered away for the rest of the service. Sure, I wanted to go in the rapture, but what if I wasn't good enough? I probably wasn't. In one of those rapture movies, I forget which one, there is a pastor who is left behind because he is just religious and doesn't have a good relationship with Jesus, even though everyone else from his congregation seems to be raptured out. Wow, if a pastor can be left behind, and he wasn't good enough, what makes me think that I'm good enough? I thought I probably wasn't, and this mark of the beast stuff sure sounded scary—I better have a plan in place just in case God decides I'm too much of a sinner to rapture out. Maybe I was just religious too; how am I supposed to know the difference? When I pray, I don't hear Jesus reply audibly to my prayers; maybe I'm supposed to if we have a good relationship? Maybe I'm in trouble? So, I thought about what I would do if and when I was left behind. It seemed like the problem in the rapture movies was that the newly saved Christians didn't go underground enough, and they either didn't arm themselves, or if they did, they didn't do it well enough. Either that or they were trying to be heroes and take on the antichrist directly instead of hiding in the shadows and waiting it out until Jesus came back for his leftovers. So, I imagined the scenarios: would I have an underground bunker? Only if I was rich, but maybe I could live in a cave or out in the woods. Then I thought, would it be better to live as a hermit or in community? Being a hermit would be lonely, but no one could betray you, and you would be less noticeable to the authorities. On the flipside, living in community would be less lonely: you could share resources, you could fight as a battalion. (I guess we can kill people because if they took the mark of the beast they're damned already anyway—yikes that's some disgusting justification.) On a more positive note: if we lived in a community we could still have church services to make it more likely that we become worthy enough to go to heaven this time around. I cringe now at the kinds of thoughts this dispensationalist theology got me thinking about. In fairness to Pastor George, my thoughts came more from the novels and movies than his sermons. Still, these dark thoughts spiraled out of control pretty quickly, and there was nothing particularly Christian about them. And it all came from a sense of unworthiness—being a wretched sinner, a lowly worm, all the self-loathing that comes from the doctrine of original sin. And Pentecostals certainly believe in that.

Talk to anyone who grew up in any type of conservative Christianity in the late nineties and early 2000s and you'll hear a familiar story. I've heard it from lots of people who had an experience I'm about to describe—doesn't matter whether you were Pentecostal, evangelical, fundamentalist, Southern Baptist, etc.: the experience of being home alone and/or unable to find your family members, but maybe they're in the bathroom or something.

(But I lived in a trailer: how hard is it really to find someone in a trailer?) You start looking in different rooms, you look outside. Is Mom's car there? You look out towards the road: are there any stalled vehicles or crashes from the people who heard the trumpet call while they were driving? Did the rapture just happen, and I got left behind? If you didn't grow up in this kind of Christianity, what I just described sounds ridiculous; indeed, it sounds ridiculous to me now. But I can't tell you how many other conservative Christians I heard similar stories from, and it happened to me several times. Being home alone, especially if you think someone else is supposed to be there or if you simply don't see them, you start to panic. You might even say a prayer: "Jesus, if the rapture just happened, and you didn't take me, please forgive my sins, and take me too. I don't want to be left behind. I know I never heard anything about last-minute repentance and a second wave of the almost good enough, but maybe, Jesus, you can make an exception for me, pretty please, amen. Oh, there's Mom outside taking out the garbage; never mind, Jesus, silly me. Forgive me of my sins anyway though, even though I can't think of any at the moment. I probably did something bad recently." Anyway, you get the idea.

The other thing about Christ's second coming was actually wanting him to hold off for a while. I know this sounds terrible; I wanted Jesus to come back, and I wanted to go in the rapture. But I also wanted to grow up and do all the things. I was just a kid after all. I wanted to see what it was like to be an adult. Heck, I hadn't even had a girlfriend yet, or been kissed, or anything interesting as far as I was concerned. I wanted to get married, do the things that married people got to do (you know what I'm talking about), get a cool job, too, like being a professional baseball player (that's what I wanted to do when I was a little kid) or be in a rock band (that's what I wanted to do as a big kid—such realistic career goals). If Jesus came back too soon, I would have only ever gotten to be a kid. Would I be stuck as a kid forever in heaven? That sounded boring: who would take me seriously? I would spend all eternity having youth fundraisers and playing silly games. I wouldn't ever get to do anything cool or important. So, take your time Jesus, let me grow up a little first, then you can come back. Just let me get to my adult years, but you can definitely come back before I'm an old man, and then I won't have to deal with old-people stuff like backaches, surgeries, illness, or nursing homes. In fact, why don't you go ahead and plan for that Jesus, before I'm fifty, who wants to be any older than that? (That's in ten years, so good thing that's not how I feel about it anymore.) This unhealthy eschatology,[1] as you can see, led to some very strange, and neurotic thoughts. Now, am I saying that everyone who has this kind of theology is mentally unwell? No. I know some very good, wise folks who would call themselves dispensationalists who never expressed any thoughts like I've described. Perhaps, with my not fully developed prefrontal cortex[2] as a young person, I was more susceptible to these day-dreams of doomsday planning. I can't say with certainty due to the passage of time, but I think Pastor George's theology wasn't so full of angst as my own childhood/teenage thoughts on the coming apocalypse. Like fear of the devil, fear of the end times was something church provided the mate-rial for, and my imagination did the rest.

I really don't think I was quite well mentally and emotionally as a child through my teen years, and maybe a little beyond that into my early twenties. There are things I can't explain, like my fear of rejection, that left me paralyzed to even make the slightest attempt at any kind of romantic relationship, which was only finally cured due to the advent of online dat-ing, where I met my wife, Jane.[3] Jane could tell you how I was very shy at first and had to be prompted for things like hand-holding and saying "I love you." I got better with these things over time. Also, if we go back earlier, to childhood, I was the same way with friendships. I was willing to be friends with anyone, but I had to be chosen; I wouldn't put myself out there. If no one talked to me first I would wander the playground by my-self, going from swing to slide to aimless meandering. I remember day care was especially boring and lonely during the summer with long hours of navigating the loneliness of the crowded playground, unwilling or unable to initiate social contact even though there were kids everywhere. I longed for the movies when they brought us inside and we watched non-age-appropriate classics such as *Wayne's World*, *Ace Ventura: Pet Detective*, *The*

---

1. Theologian Alister McGrath says, The word "eschatology" is used to refer to Christian teachings about the "last things." Just as "Christology" refers to the Christian understanding of the nature and identity of Jesus Christ, so "eschatology" refers to the Christian understanding of such things as heaven and eternal life.

The eschatology of the New Testament is complex. However, one of its leading themes is that something which happened in the past has inaugurated something new, which will reach its final consummation in the future. The Christian believer is thus caught up in this tension between the "now" and the "not yet." (McGrath, *Theology*, 123–24)

2. Kolk and Rakic, "Development of Prefrontal Cortex."

3. We met on christiandatingforfree.com so right away we knew two things about each other: we were both Christian and we appreciated a bargain, or rather—if it's free, it's for me.

Mask, Beetlejuice, and *Dumb and Dumber.* I somehow biased Jane against day care every time one of these movies was mentioned and I chimed in with, oh yeah, I watched that movie at day care when I was like seven or eight. She since has worked at a day care and is now biased against them for different reasons, so I don't think our kids will ever go to day care. Anyway, I was a lonely, socially awkward child. I probably can't pin that on Pentecostalism, but the added anxiety of looking over my shoulder for the devil, and later the existential dread of the end times, probably didn't help my fragile psyche. Maybe there is more here that has to do with having divorced parents and an initial instability in housing (to my memory we never had food insecurity). Later on, there was distrust of Dad, who would come around just to ask Mom to marry him again. (When Rebecca and I were older we often pretended not to be home when Dad stopped by and we were home alone, which is not easy to do in a trailer, and I suspect that sometimes he knew we were in there if we had been loud enough prior to his knocking on the door.) I guess I had a strange childhood that gave me anxiety, a wandering mind that didn't pay attention in school, a lack of motivation to do schoolwork, and social awkwardness. (I remember a time in sixth grade when we were told to get into groups for a project and I didn't join one because each group that had someone I at least sort of talked to was already full, so I just sat by myself in what the teacher seemed to take as an act of defiance. So, I got called out to the hall to be told by him that I had to follow instructions and I couldn't work by myself when I was told to do group work. I remember involuntary tears, which seemed to take him by surprise, and he quickly brought me back in the room and assigned me to a group. I doubt very much that I contributed a whole lot, but that was my norm anyway.) So, there was a lot going on with me, I suppose, beyond just feeling different because of Pentecostalism.

I really only felt any embarrassment over the uniqueness of my church in high school after my friends' reactions. But I do think that I needed more positive things to think about. Maybe all that exposure to talk about Satan, demon possession, homes that needed cleansed because there were demons hanging around—all these odd stories that were either in sermons, testimonies, or conversations—went a long way to making me into a fearful child. Sure, God being bigger and the devil having to flee at the name of Jesus were always emphasized. But a child's mind latches on to the weird and scary parts; the safety of Jesus doesn't get the mind racing in quite the same way as the paranoia did. Sure, when you're scared you remember to say the name of Jesus, pray in tongues, and tell Satan to flee—you do all of those things as a child. But then instead of Satan fleeing, you flee yourself to go wake up your mom and tell her you're scared and ask to sleep in her room, and you want the light on because if you sleep in the dark you'll see shadows and dark shapes that you won't be sure about, so you'll assume they are demons rather than your stuffed animal or your winter coat. Eventually, you learn to overcome this fear. Well, sort of. More so you learn that it is not acceptable to wake up your mother every night and you should just get over your fear yourself, so instead of sleeping you read a book, maybe even your Bible if you're scared enough: "The devil wouldn't attack me while I have a Bible in my hands, I'll throw this heavy King James Bible right at his head if he dares." Or you get older and now you have a Sega Genesis in your room so you can really distract your mind with a baseball game or Sonic the Hedgehog—and the devil is temporarily an afterthought. Later you get a little older and you move on by adding more abstract fears: the end times, sin (not being good enough to deserve being raptured with the rest of your family), delusions about people reading your mind, loneliness and never getting over shyness (never finding love), not having friends and wanting to go somewhere/anywhere else,[4] not being cool or accepted, and "Darn it, I'm still leaving the light on and scrutinizing shadows to make sure it's not a demon even though I'm a teenager." This is all the baggage I brought with me into early adulthood. As you can imagine I was ready to start shedding this baggage, to be someone new and different—to become my own man, make my own decisions—and I would, which is what the next chapter is really about.

4. Thankfully by high school this improved; prior to high school I was begging to go to Christian school, figuring anywhere had to be better than here.

Chapter 7: **Too Much Noise and Chaos**

Praise him with trumpet sound;
praise him with lute and harp!
Praise him with tambourine and dance;
praise him with strings and pipe!
Praise him with clanging cymbals;
praise him with loud clashing cymbals!
Let everything that breathes praise the Lord!
Praise the Lord!

—PSALM 150:3–6

MY CHILDHOOD CHURCH ENDED after the death of Pastor George. In his last months the church had shrunk and become a house church, with only a faithful few in attendance, which included my family. When it ended, we weren't sure where we were going to go; we didn't have a plan. Mom found out about a church that a few of our folks were checking out. It was in an old one-room schoolhouse; I have no idea how this building still existed and was now used for a new church. Restroom facilities were porta potties outside, which recalled our old church's early days at the barn before plumbing was installed. The pastor was a woman, Debra, but she didn't preach very often—less than once a month. She seemed to see herself more as a facilitator than a pastor. It makes me wonder now whether she had doubts about women in ministry, because there was almost always a guest preacher, and either all or most of them were men. I don't remember any other women preachers there. In fact, most of these men were regular guest preachers, and it seemed like some of them must have been on a regular rotation. I kind of think Pastor Debra only preached when she couldn't line up a speaker; it was that infrequent. I remember very little about her sermons. I probably only heard two or three, definitely not more than five.

Rebecca and I weren't fans. It was way out in the country in a different part of the county, and it took at least a half an hour to drive there, although I think it was closer to forty minutes. The people were nice but were also a little strange. I remember they had a weird thing about feathers. Pastor Debra mentioned finding a feather, I guess it was a dove feather, or she thought it was, and it reminded her that the Holy Spirit was with her. Pretty soon the whole congregation was finding feathers and giving testimonies about it. Rebecca and I made fun of them for this, and it was one of the factors that had us looking for church elsewhere, as well as the fact that we were the only youth. We found our own trendier Pentecostal church; it wasn't a megachurch, but it was a church that was trying to do all the cool stuff. I think they even had a mini skate park. They had the most up-to-date praise and contemporary songs with a rock band–like worship team. It was kind of hard to believe that Rebecca and I actually had our own church that we picked ourselves, while Mom was still worshiping with the feather-collecting rednecks. I don't think she was ever that satisfied with this church either, but it was what she had at the moment. Oddly enough, I don't know if this church even had a name; there was no sign out front. No use for a name (I'm just kidding, that's a punk band, not a church). I guess the twenty to thirty people there must have come by word of mouth like we had. Reflecting back on it now, in some ways it wasn't a bad church for what it was. There was variety in the speakers—even a messianic Rabbi was one of the guest preachers with some regularity, along with his sons; they would sing songs in Hebrew. He was probably the best of the lot. There was an odd, yet entertaining speaker named Brother Harold, a good old boy farmer and evangelist who would have interesting tangential stories that I remember now, but not how they tied into the sermon if they actually did. There was one story about going to a Chinese buffet and the only thing he wanted was king crab legs, and he kept going back just for them, eating nothing else. It annoyed the waitstaff and the other patrons, but Brother Harold said he knew what he liked and the reason he was there, so he was just going to keep going back for crab legs, and everyone would just have to get over it. Yes, all preachers like to have good stories, but we hope that you remember the point we are illustrating rather than the silly story that on its own just makes us look goofy. Like Brother Harold, I'm fond of self-deprecating humor, but if you tell a five-minute-long story and don't do a good job weaving it into the Scripture, the only thing people remember is that you're a goober.

So, Rebecca and I went to our own church for a while, and also, we did the same on our first attempt at college when we moved to Pittsburgh for art school. I won't say much about that, other than that as a video production major I realized I hated working with technology, and Rebecca had a boyfriend who died tragically at the age of twenty-two, so we went back home and took a break from school. While we were there in Pittsburgh, we went to a megachurch because it was in walking distance. We never sat next to the same person twice, certainly didn't get to know anyone. That's the last time I ever went to a megachurch, other than events like funerals or weddings. Not quite sure why people like these churches, although Rebecca goes to one now; guess I should ask her.

Sometime after our stint in Pittsburgh, Mom met Curtis, who became our stepdad. I don't remember if they met at Mom's church, Curtis's church, or a different one, but there was some sort of extra service; maybe it was a revival where people from different congregations all came together. At first Mom wasn't sure how she felt about Curtis; he was a little older, and he had a unique sense of humor. Rebecca and I weren't sure either, we were initially skeptical, but Mom hadn't dated anyone since she had divorced Dad forever ago. Ultimately, we decided we were happy for them and were supportive of the relationship.

As stated, Curtis attended his own church, which was Pentecostal/nondenominational. His church had a prison ministry, which is how Pastor Joe began—originally he was visiting prisoners and preaching to them, and then he felt called to start a halfway house for men getting out of prison and a church geared towards them. This made for an interesting dynamic, with a significant portion of parishioners being men recently released from incarceration. Curtis volunteered to manage the halfway house; he did this work for the church as well as his full-time job as a forklift operator. Mom and Curtis told us about the church and how there were actually young people there (not just the men from the house, although some of them were our age). Our main peer group, besides the fluctuating group of men from the "house," were two traditional Mennonites a few years older than us: Charity, who would eventually be Rebecca's roommate, and Mary. They both still wore head coverings and traditional dresses or long skirts. Charity would eventually abandon her Mennonite attire, while Mary never would—even though I don't know that she would still call herself Mennonite. I never did figure out how they ended up at a Pentecostal church, except for the fact that Charity seemed to be already on a course to get away from her traditional upbringing; maybe Mary was too, to a lesser extent. There were also two brothers originally from Ghana. Trent, the older brother, still had a little bit of an accent; the younger brother, Nathan, did not. Then there was DJ, a guy in his mid-twenties from Texas who played guitar. This unlikely core group formed, along with others, and we were satisfied that we had found our new church. We interacted a whole lot more with them than we had with the people in the new trendy church we found on our own. It was a return to the family feeling of church. Our conversations and relationships went deeper than a simple greeting and "See you next Sunday," which was all we managed at our previous church, where we had remained outsiders (but at least we liked it stylistically compared to that weird country church Mom was going to). But now the family was back to church together, and Mom added a boyfriend to the mix, which was new and different. At the time, he still had his own manager's quarters at the halfway house, the only real perk to his volunteer position; then again, not all of his housemates were the most trustworthy, so I guess calling his free housing a perk might be debatable—not to mention his being on call at all hours. Then again, we liked most of the men in the program and were usually surprised and disappointed whenever one of them left the program, whether because they were moving on, getting kicked out, or getting locked up all over again (the problem of recidivism—when people get stuck in a cycle, going back to prison, often for the same thing, especially if it's drug related). There were plenty who went through the revolving door.

Rebecca and I liked this church overall; it wasn't perfect, but it was a return to that family feeling of church we were used to. Mom also liked it initially but would get into disagreements with Pastor Joe on several issues. For one, he didn't seem to appreciate being challenged by a woman. He had more traditional views on women in leadership and ministry, which wasn't a problem we ever had at our old church, where women were in some leadership roles—with worship, intercessory prayer, occasional preaching, and youth ministry—but were not deacons or elders. This would eventually lead to Mom and Curtis leaving the church after Rebecca and I already had. (But we primarily left due to being in college; however, as I will discuss shortly, I was about to leave Pentecostalism for good.) One of the issues

Rebecca and I had with our new church was around the chaotic feel to worship. Sure, there were the same old problems of random people who liked to hear themselves talk, whether they were speaking English or tongues, and it became tiresome. Why should I care what this random person has to say, because it's a word from the Holy Spirit? Yeah, sure it is—who knew the Holy Spirit was so loquacious? Besides the same old nonsense, our guitar-playing buddy, DJ, usually did a fair to middling job as worship leader, at least until the Spirit got ahold of him and he would just start strumming randomly, repeating something basic like "Praise you Jesus," "Thank you Lord," or "We're crying out to you Lord Jesus." At this point Rebecca and I would usually sit down: it's going to be a while before we move on to anything else, like an actual song or a prayer. Usually this spontaneous yet repetitious worship would lead into what Rebecca and I referred to as the "yell to God" portion of the service. Usually, other people would join in the praising with DJ; speaking loudly in tongues was also prevalent, while others would yell the same type of basic praises, and they seemed to compete to see who could be the loudest. Thank God that, other than DJ, they didn't have microphones, or we would have all gone deaf in the cacophony.

This wasn't the sort of thing Rebecca and I would have willingly participated in. When we were young, if there was a wild worship moment we might raise our hands half-heartedly to show that we were participating, at least a little bit. Once, when Fran was in children's ministry, she was sitting behind Rebecca and me, and she told us to raise our hands. Praise the Lord you slackers—she didn't actually say that, but that's essentially what she said. I don't think our worship would mean very much being compulsory, but what can you do? (I think this only ever happened once, but it was obviously memorable.) Anyway, we weren't fans of the "yell to God" thing and we would get impatient any time it seemed to drag on forever. Like, come on Pastor Joe, tell DJ to get on with it; we're fine with long services if something is actually happening, but this whole "yell to God" business feels like a waste of time—they're not saying anything substantive.

While I didn't have theological differences with the church yet, I was starting to have ecclesial issues with it as far as how the service was run. I was increasingly becoming irritated with all the noise and chaos. Yet, I was raised to respect authority, especially church authority above all others. So, I kept my complaints to myself, or at least I only verbalized them to my family. I would never have even considered complaining to Pastor Joe. Besides, some of the worst noisy offenders were my friends. I wouldn't have been openly critical of them, I just wished they would tone it down and that someone would tell DJ to cut off the spontaneous praise to five minutes; no one needs twenty minutes of that—it's redundant, especially when it happens every Sunday. Maybe DJ needed a thesaurus, I don't know. I liked him as a person, and he was alright as a worship leader when he was focused and on task, but he would just go on and on with boisterous banality.

Despite my critical thoughts, I stuck around. I hadn't really grasped the fact that I had options and could make my own choice. The one time Rebecca and I had tried something else it wasn't that great either, and it took a church full of feather collectors to spur us on to finding something ourselves. We wouldn't have done it if Mom's church was even slightly more to our liking. Going into adulthood was a process with no clear defining moment for me. Sure, I could kind of listen to the music I wanted to, but it was still kind of hidden, not in the open. I was in and out of college, without a clear conception of what I wanted to do. I didn't have much experience with work, mostly just part-time stuff that wasn't any different than jobs I could have worked as a high school student. Adulthood just felt like an illusion, with nothing to clearly mark it. I didn't even try alcohol until I was twenty-two when Johnny turned twenty-one. We were in the same grade, but I was on the older end, and he was on the younger. Due to the way I was raised, I wouldn't even have thought about drinking. It wasn't even that I was strongly opposed; I just didn't really think about it one way or the other. The same was true of smoking. When I was sixteen or seventeen and working at McDonalds, I found an unused cigarette next to the cash register that one of my co-workers had left behind. I pocketed it, figuring Rebecca and I could try it later. By the time I got home I thought to myself, smoking is stupid, I don't want lung cancer, so I just threw the cigarette away without trying it and never thought about smoking again. So, given these milestones some people have and I didn't (obviously from the end of last chapter, you know I was a virgin), the only thing that marked adulthood that I can think of is the time that I voted in my first election in 2004 at the age of eighteen. All my high school friends liked John Kerry. I was still drawing anarchy symbols on stuff, so my friends were like, oh right, Phil, you're an anarchist, you probably didn't vote. Little did they know I voted, the only time in my life that I voted in a presidential general election for a Republican, George W. Bush—never again though. So, that wasn't even an adult marker I was proud of, as I became a Democrat shortly thereafter as I thought the Middle Eastern forever wars were stupid. Yes, I've also been an independent, and I briefly returned to the Republican party, voting for Larry Hogan for governor of Maryland, which was fine, but I quickly regretted becoming a Republican for reasons that anyone can guess. (I'm a pastor, so I'm not really supposed to talk about partisan politics; I'm only doing it because it relates to this chapter.) Anyway, this isn't a book about politics, and you shouldn't hate me: I've been Republican, Democrat, and independent, so you can all relate to me, right? All the hate and tribalism around politics is stupid anyway. Who cares what party you are? We're all just people trying to live our best lives.

Around this time, trying to navigate being an adult and figure out what to do with my life, I would get onto a new trajectory that would change my whole course. After leaving art school I eventually found my way to community college as an education major. Odd choice for someone who hated school and had a GED instead of a standard diploma, but I figured I could help kids like me, and it seemed like a safe choice that many of my friends had also opted for. Anyway, I had to pick something; education seemed as good a major as any.

Also, at this time, Rebecca and I wanted to connect more with our church friends and other young adults who occasionally found their way into our church. We had the idea of starting a young adults' group. We approached Pastor Joe with the idea, and he thought it sounded good, so we started the group. It was basically like a Sunday school or Bible study that met after the service. Each of the founding members would take turns leading the group, creating a lesson to share with everyone. It was at this time that I really got into reading the Bible. I hadn't been much of a Bible reader before; I would just read it every now and then when I was feeling guilty for not reading it very much. But now I found that I actually enjoyed reading the Bible and leading the group. As someone who was always shy, I was surprised that I was any good at it, but I seemed to do okay, and we had good discussions. This was when I first felt a call to ministry. There was no dramatic moment, like Pentecostals typically expect; it was just a simple sense of maybe this is what I should be doing. I talked to Pastor Joe about it, and he seemed supportive, so I started applying to transfer to a Christian college as a biblical studies major. I applied to several around Philly; I figured I had already done Pittsburgh, and I didn't want to stay local because that's boring. I remember one of my admissions interviews with one of the schools I applied at but didn't choose. One of the questions on the application was "Why did you apply at our institution?" Like a good Pentecostal, I gave a good Pentecostal answer: "Because God told me to." The admissions counselor asked me about my answer to that question, and I didn't have a good reply. I was just like, "Well God didn't literally tell me to apply here. I just felt called to ministry and this is one of the schools that looked like a good option." Ultimately, I ended up choosing Eastern University, known for Tony Campolo, Shane Claiborne, and Bryan Stevenson. It ended up being a great fit. But I would only be there a year, because my private student loans were denied for the next year. I could have covered the tuition with grants and federal loans, but there was no way to pay for housing. I briefly consider buying an RV or an old Volkswagen van, or couch surfing in various friends' dorms. I also considered the Navy for funding but eventually transferred to Millersville University in Lancaster County and commuted from home.

But I'm getting ahead of myself. My year at Eastern I went in earnestly with an intention of figuring out who I was religiously. I knew I wasn't meant to be Pentecostal, although initially my only complaint with Pentecostalism was the form and style of worship. My theology was still Pentecostal, and Eastern didn't drive it out of me that fast (if they did at all—I think I did that myself). I made a plan to visit many churches from a variety of denominations, including more established forms of Pentecostalism, such as Assemblies of God; but on the other end of the spectrum, I also visited the Catholic church. Unfortunately, I didn't visit any Anabaptist churches. I thought all Anabaptists were like Mary and Charity, who I loved, but I couldn't go to church anywhere that told women how to dress. I had no idea there were Mennonites who weren't low-key Amish, and I hadn't yet heard of the Church of the Brethren, which stopped wearing funny clothes a long time ago, or rather the "garb" as we more traditionally call the funny clothes (except there are a few conservative churches and the old orders such as the German Baptist Brethren who still wear "plain clothes"). And I thought all Quakers only ever sat around in silence for their whole service and weren't allowed to chew gum (not true on either count), so I didn't visit them either. Anyway, I made a list of churches, trying to hit all the most well-known denominations. I went with a notebook to write what I liked and didn't like, and I brought my big old King James Bible. (Later at Eastern, I would learn that serious Bible scholars read *The New Oxford Annotated Bible*, in the NRSV, preferably with the Apocrypha, so that's what I got and have used ever since, although recently I have been enjoying the *Anabaptist Community Bible*.) I kept my list of churches handy: a good visit was noted, while a bad visit meant I crossed a whole denomination off my list. The Methodists and the Presbyterians were quickly crossed off, as were the Catholics. Those were churches I visited where no one talked to me; the most I got was a handshake from the pastor on my way out the door, without any recognition of being a visitor. I will say that I've had positive experiences in all three of those denominations since then—Methodist and Catholic as a visitor, Presbyterian as a member when we lived in Salisbury, Maryland, and Jane wanted to go to the same church as her twin sister Laura. But at that time, it was a quick line through the denomination: nope, don't want that one, not friendly or welcoming. One congregation represented their whole denomination. Probably not fair, but I had a lot of them to check out and no time to waste. After I got through a few of them I started repeat visits of my favorites. Pretty soon I had a top three. I was visiting an Episcopal church with two Eastern friends. I liked it a lot for how different it was, but I think I ultimately decided it was too different; it was pretty similar in style to the Catholic church except their priests were friendly and included women, not just men. I think I was also worried that if I chose the Episcopal church, I would be choosing it because my friends were there, and I wanted to make sure I chose for the right reasons. I also liked the American Baptist Church; when Eastern University (then Eastern Baptist College) was founded, it was affiliated with that denomination before they dropped their affiliation. It felt like a comfortable choice: still low church, but with a proper order to the service, and it wasn't a bunch of noise. Later on, Jane and I would join an American Baptist Church that we attended whenever we lived in York. But at the time, it didn't seem like going far enough from my roots. I was really enjoying liturgical worship, and I really wanted to go in that direction. So, the church I chose was Lutheran (ELCA: Evangelical Lutheran Church in America), and I loved it. It was the opposite of the Pentecostal Church; everything was so orderly and defined. I enjoyed the beautiful communal aspect of the liturgy—saying the prayers, creeds, and confessions together. It wasn't quite as high church as the Episcopal Church, so I felt more comfortable, yet I still had the quiet joy of the liturgy, and it felt like a thinking person's church; it wasn't so emotional.

Now, as I said, I didn't give up my Pentecostal theology right away. I remember the first or second time I visited the Episcopal church I wanted to ask the priest about the gifts of the Spirit and praying in tongues. Would that be okay in the Episcopal Church? Or at least in my prayers at home? I seriously considered asking, but then I didn't do it. I was nearing the end of my belief in that practice, and I think I knew I wouldn't be doing it much longer. I just needed to do more reading on the topic and figure out if it was real. I read a few things about it; surprisingly I read two conservative books, *The Holy Spirit* by Billy Graham, who seemed to leave the possibility open for charismatic gifts, even though he himself wasn't charismatic, and *Charismatic Chaos* by John MacArthur, who seemed to say, as the title implies, "These people are nuts!" (I might be exaggerating slightly.) Since the time that I read these books John MacArthur came out with another book called *Strange Fire*. I haven't read that one because by the time it came out, I knew that MacArthur's theology was too conservative for my liking. I recently read *Paul, the Spirit, and the People of God* by Gordon Fee, which must be about the tamest book I ever read by a Pentecostal author; he was more focused on the biblical studies than discussing Pentecostal specifics. He is a Bible scholar, so it makes sense. It's just that when I was Pentecostal, I never would have read a book by a scholar; televangelists were our published Bible authorities (who cares about some stuffy old professors even if they are Pentecostal—they sure wouldn't fit in at my church). Two other books on my radar that I haven't read yet but seem to have good reviews are *Flame of Love* by Clark Pinnock and *Pneumatology* by Veli-Matti Kärkkäinen. Yes, I know professors say never to recommend books you haven't read (see, I like professors now, but I'm not Pentecostal either). I suppose I'm not recommending them so much as telling you, the reader, that I plan to read these books whenever I get around to it. Also, Pinnock's book was referenced in Migliore's theology textbook[1] that I read for my Introduction to Theological Reflection class in seminary. Sometimes I check footnotes for interesting books to add to my reading list. I could have sworn there was a short overview of it in one of my textbooks, but I can't seem to find it. Maybe it was a different theology book that I read for fun. (Yes, I'm weird, that is something I do.)

Now that I've given you a reading list, back to my story. Not only did my reading leave me doubtful overall about speaking in tongues and charismatic gifts (I also had a theology class at Eastern, but I don't remember all the textbooks we used), but I was also meeting students with completely different theologies and backgrounds than my own. I was more influenced by my fellow students than I was by the professors, most of whom were really not that radical. Although I was taking Kent Sparks's Introduction to Old Testament class, and he was in the process of publishing his book *God's*

---

1. Migliore, *Faith Seeking Understanding*, 226.

Word in Human Words, and his lectures were largely what is in that book. Other than the influence from Dr. Sparks, I was influenced more by my friends and acquaintances, brilliant students, most of whom were theologically universalist, progressive, and from traditional denominations such as the Episcopal Church, as well as others. I think because I was starting to care a lot more about the intellectual life I was ready to jump on board with everything my friends were talking about, and I was ready to discard everything Pentecostal/charismatic (which had been in the works before college began), everything conservative, evangelical, fundamentalist, even moderate at this point in my life. I had never cared about school before, but now I wanted to be an intellectual, and I dived headfirst into learning. Sure, I have no doubt my new attitude helped my studies. But it was a reactionary move. I was jumping from one end of a polarized spectrum to the other. (I'm talking religion rather than politics; I first became a Democrat when my theology was still ultraconservative, so these things don't always overlap.) I was a new man, even though I had started Eastern with a conservative theological bias. I even remember with embarrassment that at the beginning of my first semester at Eastern I was working on a manuscript (soon to be abandoned, as usually happens with my creative writing projects, especially back then, though it looks like I've learned how to stick to a project now). It was a book critiquing most college students who I saw as living a "liberal" lifestyle. Whenever someone asked me what I was writing when they saw me scribbling away in my notebook, I told them I was writing a story making fun of liberals. This was probably confusing for them since they probably saw me in my Obama T-shirt at some point because I wore it often in the fall of 2008. But at that time in my life, I associated conservative and liberal more with lifestyle than politics. I still cringe at the thought of that manuscript and my proud pronouncement as though I were the next Glenn Beck, when really I meant to be the next C. S. Lewis or G. K. Chesterton. I guess I wasn't really all that political back then, other than the fact that I had read *The Audacity of Hope* and Obama was my guy. Besides that, I didn't really pay a lot of attention to politics. I had begun to look at pacifist writings; I don't know that I considered myself one yet, but an older White man who had been a general didn't much interest me, and I figured he would be another Bush. He had made a joke about bombing Iran[2] and I sure didn't want to see another war with a Middle Eastern country to add to the other two that needed to end. So, it wasn't a hard choice for me, even

2. Gonyea, "Jesting, McCain Sings."

though I was definitely pro-life in the summer of 2008. But single-issue voters annoyed me, as they still do. Besides, as Shane Claiborne says, pro-life should be from the womb to the tomb, or whole life, rather than just pro-birth.[3] Also, having taken Philosophy 101 at community college, I knew John Stuart Mill's utilitarian philosophy of the greatest good.[4] In voting, like anything else, you have to weigh all the variables and add them up to what is best overall—not take one issue and say it's the only issue you care about like I saw most evangelical Christians doing. I was frustrated by the lack of thought many of my family and old friends seemed to put into their voting decisions. I get it, though: there are strong feelings on both sides of that issue, yet I wish people's thinking was less one-dimensional.

This was a big turning point in my life. I was thinking about completely new ideas from a changed perspective. Naturally, I wanted to share the joy of my new intellectual life. Rebecca seemed open to my ideas, and we had good conversations; of course she was still her own person and was having her own epiphanies at the time. I may have influenced her in some areas, but certainly not all. She didn't care for the Lutheran service whenever I brought her along. Yet I would say she got a bad first impression at the first service I brought her to along with Charity and our friend Tom, who we called a hippie because he had (I think still has) long blond hair and almost always wore tie-dye T-shirts. I brought the group to the church I attended when at college and instead of giving a normal sermon, the lead pastor showed slides from a marathon she recently participated in. There was a mini sermon that went along with it, but it definitely felt more like a slideshow. I swore up and down that they had heard an atypical sermon that Sunday, but I don't think they believed me. Later, I took Rebecca to a Lutheran service at the church I attended whenever I was home for the weekend, and Rebecca said an old lady gave her a look that seemed to say, who are these hooligans sitting behind me, I hope they don't try to steal my purse! I didn't notice it, but she probably wasn't wrong. I really liked the

3. Claiborne and Campolo, *Red Letter Revolution*, 85. If you're Catholic, Pope Leo XIV, has recently said pretty much the same thing as Claiborne and Campolo. Giangrave and Burke, "Pope Leo XIV Says." Also, I haven't read it, but Shane Claiborne has a whole book on this subject if you're interested. Claiborne, *Rethinking Life*.

4. Mill, *Utilitarianism and the 1868 Speech on Capital Punishment*. By the way, I cite Mill's utilitarian philosophy. I don't think I read his speech on capital punishment. I would have disagreed with it then and certainly disagree with it now. Overall, the idea of doing something for the greatest good makes sense in a general way; that could be applied to voting for the candidate that will do the most good and the least harm in the aggregate.

pastor at that church, but the congregation was quite unfriendly; I eventually switched Lutheran churches after I left Eastern. I stayed longer than I probably would have otherwise because of how much I liked the pastor. I almost didn't mind an otherwise cold congregation.

I had good, open conversations with Rebecca, but my intellectual evangelism did not have good results on my parents. They had tolerated my Obama T-shirt and bumper sticker, as well as my studying biblical studies even though Pentecostals didn't need a degree to learn about the Bible and preach, and if anything, it was a liability and might give you a religious spirit and quench the Holy Spirit. But when they asked me what I was learning, I shared things I learned in Dr. Sparks's class as well as the things I was discussing with my new friends. They were less than impressed. We continued to have these talks, or rather arguments, every time I came home. I soon regretted trying to evangelize my parents and wished I had just kept my mouth shut. I probably spent more time alone in my room than I may otherwise have, although that is debatable because this is when I was developing into a serious reader, not just of theology but of literature—especially the classics, history, philosophy, science. I was and I am a voracious reader (now I do most of my reading at my security guard job, which is the only thing I really like about it). This seriously affected my relationship with my parents. (Well, not Dad, I didn't see him often and when I did, we rarely had serious conversations. He would either want to go down memory lane— "When you were little . . ."—or he would air his grievances about work, family, ex-wives. I was being a dutiful son; these conversations were a drag. Maybe we should have talked theology—might have been more fun.) All the arguing with my parents seemed to push us further away, and into our own corners—made us more polarized. We stopped listening to each other; it was really a sad time that I don't think any of us handled well. I think I dug in further to my positions that I may have initially held lightly, but now I had to defend them. I think we all said things we didn't really mean. So of course when I lost my private loans, the parents weren't going to cosign, as much as I begged. Now that I'm a more mature adult, I also have a negative view of cosigning, largely due to Dave Ramsey,[5] who I think knows what he's talking about when it comes to finance. Yes, I know he is a controversial figure, and I probably wouldn't agree with him much in other areas. But at the time I was devastated that they wouldn't help me with my loans. (Also, for context, my parents don't have and never have had much

5. Ramsey, *Total Money Makeover*, 24–26.

money; they may have been lower middle class at their high point, but we're a working-class family. They might have had a little savings back then, but not much. My family has more often than not lived paycheck to paycheck. I'm sure if my parents had money they would have been willing to help me with college. They did on occasion spot me a twenty—and that scale of assistance.) Then I looked at the Navy and Mom wasn't supportive of that for the usual "mom" reasons that any loving parent would have, concerned about their kid joining the military. My parents aren't pacifists, but they are worriers (worriers not warriors, except for in prayer) and so they argued against that too. At Eastern I had also become a vegan, and this earned me some good-natured ribbing from Curtis, which wasn't really a big deal, but sometimes I wasn't in the mood with everything else I had on my plate. (Not meat though—I took that off my plate. Tofu, yum!?) At the time, I was convinced that I was a vegan for ideological reasons, but another reason was for weight loss—which I think was really the main reason. Yet, I had another position to defend—not that I needed any more. (Why didn't I just join the debate club? That would have been less annoying.) I didn't stay vegan very long either before I went back to vegetarian, and not long after I met Jane (a meat-and-potatoes Mennonite) I eventually went back to eating meat. So, anyway, there were lots of things to argue about with my parents. Over time, I really did go back towards the theological center; I just needed time and had to make the choice for myself—because I lived the examined life. That's a term from existential philosophy. As Tillich says,

> Ontic and spiritual self-affirmation must be distinguished but cannot be separated. Man's being includes his relation to meanings. He is human only by understanding and shaping reality, both his world and himself, according to meanings and values.[6]

This is the existential idea of self-examination, individuation, making meaning for ourselves, because no one can do it for us. This is true whether one chooses Christianity or another path. It only means something as a conscious choice on our part. Elizabeth Lesser describes the process of individuation; she too had a difficult time in her relationship with her mother, for Lesser it was when she was going through a divorce rather than college, as in my story. Lesser says,

> The Jungians call the long journey back to the genuine self *individuation*. Popular psychology calls it *creating boundaries*. I like

6. Tillich, *Courage to Be*, 50.

the image of building a boundary between myself and other—not to create alienation, but to secure a healthy ego and a useful identity. Until we learn to separate the conflicting urges and directives within, and establish an authentic voice for ourselves, we don't know which beliefs and values are our own, and which ones were primarily adopted from our familial and cultural conditioning. We can't answer questions like "What do I really want?" We can't make wise decisions that lead to happy lives when we don't know our true self. And we can't have healthy relationships when we can't let the other person know what we want, or value, or need.[7]

By the time I was a Millersville student I was moving in the theological direction of where I am now, a theology of openness where I acknowledge the fact that I'm not especially wise, that true wisdom comes from God. Much of what is in the Bible is mystery; we don't really know how God works, and why God works—read the book of Job. So, for questions like "Is speaking in tongues real and for today?" I don't know, I lean towards it being a phenomenon of the early church that was no longer needed after the church grew and spread, the same way we see dramatic healings and miracles become less frequent. Yes, I do affirm that God still does miracles; however, they happen less often and on a smaller scale than in the New Testament, when Jesus was on earth during his ministry and his first disciples performed the same kind of works that they learned from him, which were necessary to bring people into the church. When Jesus says that we will do greater works than these in John 14:12, I have taken that to mean salvation, leading people to faith—which is greater than physical health. While I affirm miracles and healing for today, I loathe the prosperity gospel; it seems the preachers of that "gospel" are out for themselves—making money off the gullible while the prosperity trickles down about as well as it does in the economy (not at all—it all stays at the top). That's why some of these preachers are so rich: you send in your seed faith money and a nice money tree grows for the televangelists. If you're lucky they'll mail you a trinket for your generosity. You might just as well get nothing at all. I think most of those televangelists have their hand out and are prospering by fleecing the flock, the new Elmer Gantrys[8] of the world. But overall, I would describe my theology as open, because if I don't understand something, I expect God knows better than I do. If I need to know something God will reveal it, but

7. Lesser, *New American Spirituality*, 183.

8. Lewis, *Elmer Gantry*.

I'm okay in dealing with the unknown, the mystery—like our anonymous brother told us about centuries ago.[9] Also, according to Thomas Merton,

> Faith does not simply account for the unknown, tag it with a theological tag and file it away in a safe place where we do not have to worry about it. This is a falsification of the whole idea of faith. On the contrary, faith incorporates the unknown into our everyday life in a living, dynamic and actual manner. The unknown remains unknown. It is still a mystery, for it cannot cease to be one. The function of faith is not to reduce mystery to rational clarity, but to integrate the unknown and the known together in a living whole, in which we are more and more able to transcend the limitations of our external self.[10]

So, I'm still processing the mystery, the unknown; it's what I'm doing with this memoir. Trying to understand the things I cannot comprehend, to parse what is real from what is fake. I may have gone a little differently down the path of my faith journey than most of my family, but that's alright. If I am blessed to adopt children (we can't have our own), I hope they find faith that works for them. If they decide to stick with Church of the Brethren Anabaptism, then I'll be happy. If they find some other expression of Christianity then I'll also be happy, even if it's Pentecostalism. As the Brethren writer Martin Brumbaugh stated, "there is no force in religion."[11] Whatever they decide, I will trust them to make the best decision they can through both their faith and reason, and Jane and I will be here for them along the way. I don't fault Mom for choosing Pentecostalism, even though it doesn't suit me. I'm thankful for growing up rooted in the Christian faith, even though I transplanted myself into different denominations that fit the time and place.

I found the Church of the Brethren (COB) without looking for it. I was happy at the Lutheran Church when Rebecca told me about a church plant Charity had invited her to that was supposed to be mostly college students. (They were mostly from Frankin and Marshall; they were more your upper-class type of kids. I wasn't too sure about most of them at first, but they grew on me.) The Pastor had long hair and dressed casually. Worship was around tables and always included open discussion time. I loved it. I thought I was only visiting, but I stayed for a year until they moved

9. *Cloud of Unknowing.*
10. Merton, *New Seeds of Contemplation*, 136.
11. Durnbaugh, *Fruit of the Vine*, 390–91.

further into Lancaster County and I decided it was too far to drive out there every week. Then I went back to the Lutheran Church for a bit. Jane and I got engaged; I took her to my church several times. I was already into the process doing background stuff for ministry in the ELCA, but I asked Jane how she felt about Lutheranism, given that I wasn't going to be the kind of husband to say we're going to my church, and you can just be my submissive wife (Eph 5:22); rather we would decide together. Jane told me she thought the Lutheran Church was too formal. So, I said, "Okay, we'll pick a different church together." First, I tried the nearest Church of the Brethren, but they just weren't very friendly. I visited a few times and usually the only person who talked to me was an older woman who was on their welcoming committee or something like that. There were other young people, but they didn't greet me, and I was shy, as we've already established. So, I decided to keep looking. The first Sunday Jane and I visited First Baptist together it was an easy decision to stay there. Everyone was so friendly and welcomed us right away. I had remembered the American Baptist Church from my college church visits, so it was what I wanted to start with, and we both agreed there was no reason to keep looking. Jane and I weren't married yet and she was still living in Maryland. Every time I went back to First Baptist Church (FBC) they were just as friendly when I was by myself, so we stuck with it. Even though the theology there was a little too conservative for my preference, the people were amazing—good salt-of-the-earth folks who would do anything they could to lend a hand—and you sure wouldn't ever feel lonely attending there in such a welcoming environment.

Over the years we moved around a lot, including to the South, where the American Baptist Church (ABC) doesn't exist, so sometimes we had to go to other churches. We moved back to York twice, and there was never any question where we were going to go to church, and we were always treated as though we had never left as we were welcomed back. If it isn't clear by now, I think being welcoming is essential for church, and I try not to go anywhere that isn't. I suppose this comes from my church family growing up, as well as from my quiet personality. I like talking to people, and I usually test as slight extravert on the Myers Briggs personality test, yet I act more like an introvert—I have trouble initiating conversation with new people. Welcome is an essential part of church. Yes, sometimes we need to gauge whether someone wants to talk or whether they want to slip in and out quietly while they decide if they want to be part of our church; everyone is different.

Due to financial reasons, I didn't go to seminary until nine years after college. Also due to financial reasons, I chose Bethany Theological Seminary. I had visited the campus back when I was going to the COB church plant, and I remembered affordability was a big part of their mission. Brethren sold me on a bargain—how Brethren is that! Initially, I kept my American Baptist affiliation, yet I seemed to be losing my Baptist connections. Sure, I would visit FBC, the few times I was in my hometown visiting family—otherwise I wasn't very connected anymore. The congregation was changing, people I knew left, new people I didn't know joined. The pastor would later become a chaplain, and they would get a new pastor that I've never met. At first when we moved to Indiana, we went to another ABC that was within walking distance of our apartment, also called FBC (and now I know my ABC's). We liked the pastor there (nice guy with engaging style), but his theology was very Calvinist, which I don't particularly care for (I went to a Presbyterian church for two years, I gave it a fair hearing). It also seemed like the staff there was in conflict; indeed, they had complete turnover within the year, after we already left. In the meantime, I was really enjoying Brethren/Anabaptist theology at seminary, and I was positively influenced by my ministry formation professor, as well as my fellow students, to give Church of the Brethren another try. This coincided with an opportunity to do a pulpit fill at a little country church, where I then volunteered to teach adult Sunday school (the only age group they had). Sometimes I wasn't sure if this congregation was the best fit, but sometimes God has us in a place for reasons we don't understand. Of course, I did my first official internship with the Christian Church Disciples of Christ in town because it was close and slightly bigger, or rather active enough to give me work to do during the week. I kept my COB affiliation, although we were treated as members at First Christian even though we never "officially" became members. I eventually did my licensing at that small country church in South Central Indiana before becoming a pastor in Northern Indiana, while still a seminary student with two years to go at my part-time pace. My seminary journey had its ups and downs as I struggled to balance work and life, working full-time all through seminary while also engaging in ministry. I often wish I would do something the easy way for once, but I never seem to; it's been a long and winding journey, but I thank God for it. Despite all the blood, sweat, and tears.

I hope these don't come off as boring details, but it's where I am now. No, the journey isn't over. I have not reached the mountaintop of perfection,[12] nor the Omega point;[13] I'm still just doing my best to be a Christian and understand what God is calling me to. It's often not clear, but I try to prayerfully discern and make the best possible choice. Sometimes I get it wrong, I know that, but with God's help hopefully I'm on the right track at least some of the time. If you're Pentecostal and you read this book to see why some idiot would leave the best expression of Christianity, then I thank you for reading through to the end. I'm not trying to convince you that you should be in a traditional denomination because yours is too wild. If that is where God is calling you to be, bless you and your faith journey. I hope you continue to experience the presence of the Holy Spirit in the way that is most meaningful to you.

If, like me, you are an ex-Pentecostal or charismatic, I hope you found this a fair critique. If you thought it should have been mean-spirited then I'm sorry to disappoint you. Years ago, I might have written this story with a different tone. However, it is not my intention to tear anyone down or be negative. I tried to call balls and strikes as objectively as I could; no doubt, like an umpire in a baseball game, I probably didn't see everything quite right. Feel free to review the plays, since that's a thing in baseball now, and to continue the metaphor. I did my best, strictly from my own memory. All mistakes are my own. If anyone who knows me finds they are reading about themselves or someone they know, I hope they found my depictions of events true to life. Again, some things were changed, like names; there were also a lot of good stories that I chose not to tell for various reasons. Many I considered too personal to the people involved. If you think I left something important out, it was probably on purpose. It is not my intention to hurt anyone with this book, and I sincerely hope the retelling has not caused anyone pain. It was a challenge to think about some of these things I hadn't thought about in years. Many of these stories I hadn't really processed because I actively avoided it. Writing this forced me to grapple with the past, and it wasn't easy.

If this was your introduction to Pentecostalism and the charismatic movement, don't just take my word for it or consider this the be-all and end-all. This isn't even a proper theology book as it is mainly a memoir. Check it out yourself if you are interested. There are a variety of Pentecostal churches, some in formal denominations, others nondenominational. There are tiny churches and there are megachurches. There are even charismatic

---

12. Gregory of Nyssa, *Life of Moses*, 91–101.

13. Teilhard de Chardin, *Phenomenon of Man*, 257–60.

congregations in traditional denominations, including mainline and Catholic. The churches I've described in my story are of one specific type: small, independent, "storefront" Pentecostalism, or the charismatic fringe, as I've called it. There are many books you could read about Pentecostalism and the charismatic movement; I've only referenced a few, but maybe that gives you a place to start. This memoir was anecdotal, just my own experience primarily from childhood and as best as I could remember. This book in no way represents a systematic theology of Pentecostalism, nor does it pretend to. It's simply my own musings on the religion of my youth and doubles as a coming of age story. Incidentally, I don't think I could possibly write about my childhood without writing about my church and religious life; it was such an integral part of growing up. Even if I had wanted to focus the memoir on being a child of a single mother, or being a high school slacker, or being a lonely/depressed child, the church would have still had a central place in my story because my life revolved around it, and I'm ok with that. I did become a pastor, so church has always been and always will remain an important part of who I am. Sometimes I wish it wasn't, because church has been both a place of joy and pain for me. I haven't figured out how to make it exclusively a place of joy, and I don't know if it's possible, but I'm going to keep trying anyway.

Epilogue

Then afterward
I will pour out my spirit on all flesh;
your sons and your daughters shall prophesy,
your old men shall dream dreams,
and your young men shall see visions.

—JOEL 2:28

So, I THOUGHT THE epilogue of this story would be kind of like what I wrote at the end of my last chapter. I didn't really think I would have a new pertinent story that would be at all related to the topic of this memoir. Indeed, maybe I'm making a stretch as it is, or perhaps not? Had I not grown up Pentecostal, I probably would have responded to this incident in a different way; I'm almost certain of it. Yes, the story I'm about to relate is from only a few months ago in the spring of 2025 and it happened right in my Brethren Church. Let's not be hasty though—I didn't speak in tongues or prophesy; that would be weird, right? In fact, this event happened between me and my foster son on a Saturday afternoon. We'll call him Junior or JR for short because that's nice and easy. (That's not his name, let me be 100 percent clear. Privacy is very important for foster youth.)

I was having one of my office days. Yes, I have office hours on Saturday: being a multi-vocational pastor is challenging, and you have to do things when it fits your schedule—ideal or not. It's not for the faint of heart and I don't recommend it for most people. That Saturday Jane decided to take JR in to visit me while I was in the office, and we would have lunch together. As it would turn out, the quilters (probably the most active group our church still has) were working on projects in the basement. Jane had tried out quilting but didn't really stick with it; however, she still sometimes works on sewing projects when the quilters meet, so she went downstairs to meet with them while I got JR started on his lunch, one of those microwavable Gerber meals. So, I brought JR his meal. He still needed a fair amount of supervision at this point, so I usually would sit with him until he was done eating before I ate my own food, which is what I did, setting him in his high chair and sitting at the table next to him, just making sure he didn't have any issues or make too big of a mess. We were the only ones in the church fellowship hall; everyone else in the building was in the basement. Then the strangest thing happened: he started waving slightly to the right of us. I looked and the only thing there were some flowers on the table. I said, "Are you waving at the flowers, buddy?" Sometimes when he didn't have many words he would point to something he was interested in. He wouldn't typically wave though. Sure, he would wave to our cats, but not to inanimate objects. I tried to brush it off. But he was quite distracted from his food, which was odd, as he loves food. He waved several times, still looking slightly off to the right, but there was nothing there but those flowers in a vase on the table. Then JR waved and said, "Sit," in his friendly inviting way. But who was he inviting to sit with us? Then I said, "Buddy, there's no one there." Then he got a weird look on his face, kind of a confused squint like he didn't quite know what to think, and then he smeared mashed potatoes on his face. He sort of just picked at his food after that, which was also unusual for him. Thankfully, Jane finally came back upstairs, and we ate our lunch. I didn't tell her what had happened, I was still trying to figure out what the heck I had just witnessed. When we let JR out of his high chair, he went to explore a wheelbarrow with some landscaping equipment in the far left of the fellowship hall, and that had his attention for the remainder of our lunch, even though we kept telling him to quit playing with it. I went through the rest of my office day a bit distracted, a little creeped out, but determined to get all my work done. Interestingly, I had already begun writing this memoir. I was glad I was on the second chapter and that this weird event hadn't occurred while writing chapter 1, Fear of the Devil. And no, before you ask, I only wrote a tiny amount of this book in the church office, and only after I had completed all of my tasks. I estimate that I wrote one percent of this book in my office. (Actually, I wrote about seventy percent of it during Church of the Brethren Annual Conference 2025 in Greensboro, North Carolina. I came early for an ethics class—I flew, so I had time to pass at the airport—and I spent the majority of my downtime writing that entire week. It will be obvious, for those who are Brethren and know what I'm talking about: I went to zero percent of the business sessions, except once to meet up with someone, but I didn't even find them anyway.) Needless to say, that day in the office I had the heebie-jeebies, to use a weird old (well, 1970s) expression—like they might say on *Scooby Doo*. Zoinks, jinkies, jeepers! (Okay I swear I'm done being goofy.) Later, I turned on a few more lights than usual, I avoided looking towards the fellowship hall, and by the end of the day I listened to some relaxing Coldplay and Starflyer 59, when I normally work in silence because most of my jams aren't really church appropriate anyway. I tried not to think about what had just happened, but I also couldn't not think about it. The experience was bizarre: was it a ghost (which I don't and never have believed in), or a demon (which, why would there be one in our church), or was it nothing (but it didn't feel like nothing, and JR had never done anything like this before)? Could it have just been imaginary? I don't know? Why would there be an evil presence in the church—shouldn't that be the last place an evil spirit would want to hang out? It couldn't be that, but how to explain it? Imaginary friend was the best possible explanation, but why today when he never had one before? I wasn't even sure whether I was going to tell Jane or anyone about it or do anything. Plus I was trying to stay focused on my work—but that was hard to do.

When I got home, I decided that I didn't want to keep it to myself, so I told Jane what happened, and she took me seriously. I didn't have to feel like I was crazy or being weird, or at least I didn't with Jane, but now that I had told someone I kind of wanted to tell one or two of my mentors in the church and get their thoughts, maybe their assistance. One of my mentors is a retired minister who served on my mentor team for my Ministry Formation class. I wanted to talk to him, but he is more traditional, and I wasn't sure if he would feel comfortable with a conversation like this. The other, whom I did end up calling, has been a mentor in a more unofficial capacity, and we have collaborated on various new ministry ideas. But he seemed the perfect person to talk to if I was going to talk to anyone. He spent some of his young adult years with the Jesus People, so he had a charismatic phase as basically a Christian hippie. Some of his interests are still more on the mystic and unorthodox side of Christianity. He felt like the best possible person to ask, so I gave him a call and related the events. I asked if the experience I described and how I felt made sense or if I was just being paranoid. But he said no, it made sense that something like that could happen. He said little children can see things differently than adults because they are more open, that they don't have the same expectations of what they will see, physical reality versus spiritual. They don't have our adult biases as a filter for perception. He referred me to the work of Rudolf Steiner, who covered some of these topics in *Theosophy*. He writes extensively about the Spiritland and those who are able to perceive it visually (spiritual sight) and audibly (spiritual hearing, "the music of the spheres"). The Spiritland will seem fantastic to someone only willing to perceive with their physical senses[1] (i.e. adults versus children), which is my mentor's take on Steiner and how his thoughts apply to this situation. (Assuming I myself could see into the Spiritland as a child, I actively taught myself to avoid it, preferencing the physical due to my childhood phobia. That is of course assuming it's not all a bunch of delusional bs, as my highly rational brain would like me to declare to myself and the world.) Then I asked my mentor, "What should I do? Cleanse the church? Cast the demon out?" "No," he replied. "We shouldn't make assumptions about what JR saw. Next time instead of telling JR there's no one there, ask questions, be curious. Ask open questions, not leading questions, let him tell you what he sees." It was a relief to hear that I wasn't being crazy, even though I didn't really have answers as to what it was or what to do, other than wait and see if it happens again, then ask questions.

I talked to Jane about it and we both agreed that we should still do something rather than just wait and see. We thought we could at least pray in the fellowship hall ourselves. In the meantime, I was very busy, and two weeks passed before we had time to do anything. It was a Wednesday when JR had a visit with his bio mom, and we had a music and worship meeting at church. When the meeting finally ended and the last person we were chatting with left, Jane suggested getting the anointing oil from my office. I didn't know if that was necessary, but like everything else, it couldn't hurt, better safe than sorry. Maybe JR had just imagined people in the fellowship hall where they normally sit, and we were there to deal with his imaginary friends. Get out imaginary people, I want real things! This isn't *Barney and Friends*. But if there was something there that didn't belong, better tell it to get lost. I think especially after this amount of time had passed, we felt a little silly, so we made sure everyone had left, and then we prayed, because it never hurts to pray. We prayed that if there was anything there that didn't belong then it wasn't welcome there and needed to go back to wherever

1. Steiner, *Theosophy*, 101–6.

it came from. Then I put a dab of anointing oil over the doorway, and we called it good. It was a little anticlimactic. I don't know if I expected something dramatic to happen like the old stories I would hear about in my childhood church, but nothing happened. No spirits manifested in protest or asked to be cast into stray alley cats (we're in the city, so no pigs around). It was done and we felt peace, whether because we prayed or because there was never anything to worry about. It was nearly time to pick up JR from his supervised visit, so we left the church and went home for a bit before going to pick him up. We never had any more incidents, and I still don't know what to think. Yet, I still get chills when I remember. Certainly, it was strange, and I'm more comfortable just brushing it off like it never happened, the way I have with my childhood memories that are so distant and unreal. It's a mystery; I'll never know if it was real or imaginary, if I was being paranoid or prudent. I'm glad this was an isolated incident, yet there is no way to test, to confirm or deny. I didn't wait to see if JR waved at anyone else invisible and invited them to sit; there was never a repeat. I have to be okay in the not knowing, in the unexplainable, and that's often not easy. The mind wants clarity and closure, but either there was never anything there to begin with or we had authority in Christ Jesus to drive it out and it is gone. I know that last part sounds weird; I'd much rather it was only ever imaginary and a bunch of hooey.

Well, I would have been perfectly fine without a new story to put at the end of the book, but here we are. I couldn't exclude it when it seems to relate to the other phenomena described from my memories. I would much rather have written some positive experiences, like about Jesus or more about angels, but so many of my recollections are negative. It affects my propensity towards favoring the rational thinking mind and my avoidance of the spiritual realm, mystic and emotional. However, life doesn't work that way—we use all parts of ourselves, and we can't be pure reason, a brain without feeling. We are exposed to the spirit world, whatever that means; there are healthy and unhealthy ways to respond (like with anything else). I wish I could have told more positive stories, but that's why I asked my wife, Jane, to write the afterword, because she does have positive experiences to share with you. So, I hope you'll read to the end for a different perspective. There's never just one story, one single way of seeing the world. We can learn a lot from others, and I fully acknowledge that I haven't said the last word about Pentecostalism, the charismatic movement, spirituality, angels, and demons. We each have our own stories; maybe most people don't have a story on these topics, or maybe more people do than I realize. I don't speak for all ex-Pentecostals; I only speak for myself and have never claimed to have the last word or a special wisdom on the Holy Spirit and the supernatural. In fact, I'm giving the last word away, so please read the afterword, and thank you for coming along with me on this strange journey.

We covered a lot of heavy and obscure topics in this short book, and some readers may not be sure how to feel about it. So, let's recenter ourselves with a closing prayer.

> God of the universe,
>
> Your thoughts are not our thoughts,
>
> As the heavens are higher than the earth,
>
> So are your ways higher than our ways (Isa 55:8-9),
>
> Let our hearts be encouraged and united in love,
>
> Give us the riches of assured understanding,
>
> And knowledge of your mysteries in Christ,
>
> In whom is hidden all treasures of wisdom and knowledge (Col 2:2-3).
>
> Let the advocate, the Holy Spirit, teach and remind us of the things Jesus said (John 14:26).
>
> So that we will know how to live,
>
> How best to follow you through all of life's challenges and difficulties.
>
> We won't always know what is best,
>
> But we trust you to lead and guide us into your truth and wisdom.
>
> You told us to go boldly forth as you promised to never leave or forsake us (Deu 31:6).
>
> Help us as we process all of these things we read about,
>
> And the mysteries we have encountered in our own life of faith.
>
> Give us the gift of tolerance and patience with our sisters and brothers of all religious varieties.
>
> We can have our differences in theology and expression of worship and still be united in the family of God.

Let us beware of hubris, lest we fall in our pride.

But do give us the confidence to go out and explore,

To examine our faith and make it our own.

We must not fear study, facts, science, exegesis,

Instead, we must access truth where we find it.

Make use of our enquiring, curious minds, to be used for your good and the good of the world.

We ask all these things in your name, Lord Jesus Christ.

Amen[2]

---

2. In the original manuscript, I used a section of a prayer by Harry Emerson Fosdick.

Fosdick, *A Book of Public Prayer*, 34–35.

As I patiently or perhaps impatiently awaited a permissions contract I decided rather than hold up the production of the book to write my own. Not one that would copy Fosdick, but just as his prayer covered what I was thinking about that would close out my book in a satisfying way, I think my own words and those of scripture weaved in, leave us with peace and closure. I did what Mom in her Pentecostal convictions always advises, pray the scriptures, remind God of God's promises. So that's just what I did. Perhaps this is more meaningful than if I had used a prayer from a book. Before I wrote the epilogue, I hadn't consciously thought about ending with a prayer. I just happened to come across the prayer book in my office and used a different section of his prayer in a service, and I realized how much I liked it. Then I decided it was the perfect way to end my own words here. I'm glad I found it. But I think perhaps the Spirit had other ideas, and I might not have written my own prayer if I hadn't found Fosdick's first. Sometimes we just need some inspiration.

Afterword by Jane Matarese

> Beloved, do not believe every spirit, but test the spirits to see whether they are from God, for many false prophets have gone out into the world.

—1 JOHN 4:1

I'VE NEVER WRITTEN AN afterword before, so thank you for this opportunity. Great job sharing your story. Thank you for your vulnerability in sharing difficult memories.

Like Phil said, I grew up in the Mennonite church, and if you don't know anything about the Mennonites, we are very conservative. People didn't raise their hands during worship. Worship was mostly hymns. I remember there was some controversy when it was decided to add contemporary worship music one or two Sundays a month. We put the music on an overhead projector and people called it off-the-wall music.

I don't have Phil's memory for dates, but I believe it was in 2001 that my dad, the pastor of the church, went to a conference at the Toronto Airport Christian Fellowship. For those unfamiliar with that, it was a megachurch that was having an outpouring of the Holy Spirit. People were speaking in tongues and prophesying and being slain in the spirit.

When he came back, Dad wanted to share the joy he had experienced in this type of worship and tried to make changes in the church. This did not go over well, and when it was time to renew his contract, the vote came back not to do so. To be clear, I don't believe the experience Dad had was the sole reason for the outcome of the vote. However, one person did tell Dad that it was because of the charismatic leaning that he did not vote for Dad to stay the pastor. The vote was very close, and one or two votes may have made the difference.

I would eventually join Dad at several of these conferences and I loved the experience. I saw people dancing to worship music. I felt free to express myself. I really believed I could feel God's presence there in a way I had never experienced it before.

I was never sure about speaking in tongues, and the way they talked about it made me feel like I wasn't filled with the Holy Spirit if I didn't speak in tongues. I believe that speaking in tongues is one gift of the Holy Spirit but that not everyone receives the same gift.

In 2004, I went on a summer mission trip to the Philippines through Eastern Mennonite Missions. It was my first time being away from my family and my first mission trip. I had been to Canada before, but this would be something different entirely.

There were three and a half weeks of training and three and a half weeks of outreach and then a week of debriefing. The relevant story takes place during the beginning training. We usually had training twice a day, and there was worship with each training. One training day, the leader said he felt that we were supposed to just continue worshiping and not do the training that was planned.

I soon felt God's presence in the room. I sat down because I was pretty sure I was going to be slain in the Spirit, and I didn't think anyone would catch me, so I decided to sit. But then, they did a prayer circle, and I was laying down at this point. I still held people's hands even though I was on the ground. One of my team leaders was saying "fire" over me. Yelling "fire" at someone in the Spirit was a reference to the tongues of fire that alighted on the heads of the disciples on Pentecost Sunday.

While I was laying there soaking in the presence of God, I felt like His hand was on my waist and that He was saying He wanted to be my lover, not just my Father or Friend. Time was irrelevant and I was the last one in the room. I was there for two and a half or three hours.

This was unlike any other experience I had with God before. I don't even want to say that I was slain in the Spirit. I like to explain it by saying the presence of God was so real and so heavy that I couldn't stand in His presence.

There have been times over the years that I have questioned that experience, but in my heart, I know that was a one-hundred-percent real experience. The thing I have always said is that for every real thing there is a counterfeit. I believe Phil experienced a lot of counterfeits in his life and that makes me a little sad for him because that experience I had with God that day has carried me through when I doubted my relationship with Him.

Bibliography

Adams, Douglas. *The Ultimate Hitchhiker's Guide to the Galaxy*. New York: Del Rey, 2002.

Adler, Alfred. *The Individual Psychology of Alfred Adler: A Systematic Presentation in Selections from His Writings*. Edited by Heinz L. Ansbacher and Rowena Ansbacher. New York: Harper & Row, 1956.

AFI. "I Wanna Get a Mohawk (But Mom Won't Let Me Get One)." *Answer That and Stay Fashionable*. Nitro, 1995, compact disc.

Athanasius. *The Life of Anthony and the Letter to Marcellinus*. Translated by Robert C. Gregg. Mahwah, NJ: Paulist, 1980.

Barth, Karl. *The Faith of the Church: A Commentary on the Apostles Creed According to Calvin's Catechism*. Translated by Gabriel Vahanian. New York: Living Age, 1958.

Bass, Diana Butler. *Christianity for the Rest of Us: How the Neighborhood Church Is Transforming the Faith*. San Francisco: HarperSanFrancisco, 2006.

Bonaventure. *The Life of St. Francis*. In *The Soul's Journey into God; The Tree of Life; The Life of St. Francis*, 177–327. Translated by Ewert Cousins. New York: Paulist, 1978.

Brown, Dale W. *Another Way of Believing: A Brethren Theology*. Elgin, IL: Brethren, 2005.

Burge, Ryan P. *The Nones: Where They Came From, Who They Are, and Where They Are Going*. Minneapolis: Fortress, 2021.

Claiborne, Shane. *Rethinking Life: Embracing the Sacredness of Every Person*. Grand Rapids: Zondervan, 2023.

Claiborne, Shane, and Tony Campolo. *Red Letter Revolution: What If Jesus Really Meant What He Said?* Nashville: Nelson, 2012.

The Cloud of Unknowing: With the Book of Privy Counsel. Translated by Carmen Acevedo Butcher. Boulder, CO: Shambhala, 2009.

Dashboard Confessional. "Screaming Infidelities." *The Places You Have Come to Fear the Most*. Vagrant, 2001, compact disc.

DC Talk. "Jesus Freak." *Jesus Freak*. ForeFront, 1995, compact disc.

DeGroat, Chuck. *When Narcissism Comes to Church: Healing Your Community from Emotional and Spiritual Abuse*. Downers Grove, IL: InterVarsity, 2020.

Durnbaugh, Donald F. *Fruit of the Vine: A History of the Brethren 1708–1995*. Elgin, IL: Brethren, 1997.

Fee, Gordon D. *Paul, the Spirit, and the People of God*. Peabody, MA: Hendrickson, 1996.

Fosdick, Harry Emerson. *A Book of Public Prayer*. New York: Harper & Brothers, 1959.

The Get Up Kids. "Ten Minutes." *Eudora*. Vagrant, 2001, compact disc.

Giangrave, Claire, and Daniel Burke. "Pope Leo XIV Says 'Inhuman Treatment of Immigrants' in the U.S. Isn't 'Pro-Life.'" *NPR*, Oct. 1, 2025. https://www.npr.org/2025/10/01/nx-s1-5560169/pope-leo-xiv-says-inhuman-treatment-of-immigrants-in-the-u-s-isnt-pro-life.

Goldfinger. "My Girlfriend's Shower Sucks." *Goldfinger*. Mojo, 1996, compact disc.

Gonyea, Don. "Jesting, McCain Sings: 'Bomb, Bomb, Bomb' Iran." *NPR*, Apr. 20, 2007. https://www.npr.org/2007/04/20/9688222/jesting-mccain-sings-bomb-bomb-bomb-iran.

Graham, Billy. *The Holy Spirit*. Nashville: W Pub Group, 1997.

Gregory of Nyssa. *The Life of Moses*. Translated by Abraham J. Malherbe and Everett Ferguson. Mahwah, NJ: Paulist, 1978.

Hammond, Frank, and Ida Mae Hammond. *Pigs in the Parlor: A Practical Guide to Deliverance*. Kirkwood, MO: Impact, 2010.

Hananoki, Eric. "Pat Robertson Warns Against Harry Potter, TV Witchcraft, and 'Demonic' Ouija Boards." *Media Matters*, July 18, 2011. https://www.mediamatters.org/pat-robertson/pat-robertson-warns-against-harry-potter-tv-witchcraft-and-demonic-ouija-boards.

Julian of Norwich. *Showings*. Translated by Edmund Colledge and James Walsh. Mahwah, NJ: Paulist, 1978.

Jung, Carl. *Memories, Dreams, Reflections*. Edited by Aniela Jaffé. Translated by Richard and Clara Winston. New York: Vintage, 1989.

Kärkkäinen, Veli-Matti. *Pneumatology: The Holy Spirit in Ecumenical, International, and Contextual Perspective*. Grand Rapids: Baker, 2002.

Klein, Naomi. *No Logo: Taking Aim at Brand Bullies*. New York: Picador, 1999.

Kolk, Sharon M., and Pasko Rakic. "Development of Prefrontal Cortex." *Neuropsychopharmacol* 47 (2022) 41–57. https://www.nature.com/articles/s41386-021-01137-9.

Lee, Morgan. "Teen Mania: Why We're Shutting Down After 30 Years of Acquire the Fire." *Christianity Today*, Dec. 17, 2015. https://www.christianitytoday.com/2015/12/teen-mania-why-shutting-down-acquire-fire-ron-luce/.

Lesser, Elizabeth. *The New American Spirituality: A Seeker's Guide*. New York: Random House, 1999.

Lewis, C. S. *The Screwtape Letters*. San Francisco: HarperSanFrancisco, 1996.

Lewis, Sinclair. *Elmer Gantry*. New York: Signet, 2007.

Liardon, Roberts. *God's Generals*. Video series. Sarasota, FL: Roberts Liardon Ministries, 1998. Videocassette (VHS), 12 tapes, 60 min. each.

MacArthur, John. *Charismatic Chaos*. Nashville: Nelson, 1993.

———. *Strange Fire: The Danger of Offending the Holy Spirit with Counterfeit Worship*. Nashville: Nelson, 2013.

Mewithoutyou. "Torches Together." *Catch for Us the Foxes*. Tooth & Nail, 2004, compact disc.

McGrath, Alister E. *Theology: The Basics*. Oxford: Blackwell, 2004.

McKim, Donald K. *The Westminster Dictionary of Theological Terms*. Louisville: Westminster John Knox, 2014.

McLaren, Brian. *A Generous Orthodoxy: Why I Am a Missional, Evangelical, Post/Protestant, Liberal/Conservative, Mystical/Poetic, Biblical, Charismatic/Contemplative, Funda-*

mentalist/Calvinist, Anabaptist/Anglican, Methodist, Catholic, Green, Incarnational, Depressed-Yet-Hopeful, Emergent, Unfinished Christian. Grand Rapids: Zondervan, 2004.

Merton, Thomas. *New Seeds of Contemplation.* New York: New Directions, 1961.

Migliore, Daniel L. *Faith Seeking Understanding: An Introduction to Christian Theology.* Grand Rapids: Eerdmans, 2004.

Mill, John Stuart. *Utilitarianism and the 1868 Speech on Capital Punishment.* Indianapolis: Hackett, 2002.

Millencolin. "No Cigar." *Pennybridge Pioneers.* Epitaph, 2000, compact disc.

Obama, Barack. *The Audacity of Hope: Thoughts on Reclaiming the American Dream.* New York: Three Rivers, 2006.

Okey, Thomas, trans. *The Little Flowers of Saint Francis.* Mineola, NY: Dover, 2003.

Fountain, Lauren, and Anis Rehman. "Nightmares in Children." *Sleep Foundation,* Nov. 8, 2023. https://www.sleepfoundation.org/nightmares/nightmares-in-children.

Pettit, Mike. *Raised by Wolves: Growing Up Poor in 1950's America.* Self-published, CreateSpace, 2017.

Pinnock, Clark H. *Flame of Love: A Theology of the Holy Spirit.* Downers Grove, IL: InterVarsity, 1999.

Ramsey, Dave. *The Total Money Makeover: A Proven Plan for Financial Fitness.* Nashville: Nelson, 2009.

Rauschenbusch, Walter. *Christianity and the Social Crisis in the 21st Century.* Edited by Paul Raushenbush. New York: HarperOne, 2007.

Rowling, J. K. *Harry Potter and the Prisoner of Azkaban.* New York: Scholastic, 1999.

Russell, Bertrand. *The Problems of Philosophy.* London: Oxford University Press, 1978.

Sartre, Jean-Paul. "Existentialism." In *A Casebook on Existentialism,* edited by William V. Spanos, 275–97. New York: Thomas Y. Crowell, 1966.

Saves the Day. "My Sweet Fracture." *Through Being Cool.* Equal Vision, 1999, compact disc.

Sparks, Kenton L. *God's Word in Human Words: An Evangelical Appropriation of Critical Biblical Scholarship.* Grand Rapids: Baker, 2008.

Specter, Ian. *The Truth About Chuck Norris: 400 Facts About the World's Greatest Human.* New York: Gotham, 2007.

Steiner, Rudolf. *Theosophy: An Introduction to the Supersensible Knowledge of the World and the Destination of Man.* Translated by Henry B. Monges and Gilbert Church. Hudson, NY: Anthroposophic, 1971.

Street Dogs. "Two Angry Kids." *State of Grace.* Hellcat, 2008, compact disc.

Suicidal Tendencies. "Institutionalized." *Suicidal Tendencies.* Frontier, 1983, compact disc.

Teilhard de Chardin, Pierre. *The Phenomenon of Man.* New York: Harper & Row, 1965.

Teresa of Avila. *Teresa of Avila: Selections from The Interior Castle.* Edited by Emilie Griffin. Translated by Kieran Kavanaugh. San Francisco: HarperSanFrancisco, 2004.

Tillich, Paul. *The Courage to Be.* New Haven: Yale University Press, 2000.

———. *Systematic Theology.* Vol. 2: *Existence and the Christ.* Chicago: University of Chicago Press, 1957.

The Vandals. "An Idea for a Movie." *Hitler Bad, Vandals Good.* Nitro, 1998, compact disc.

Ward, Benedicta, trans. *The Sayings of the Desert Fathers.* London: A. R. Mowbray, 1975.

Weezer. "My Name Is Jonas." *Weezer (Blue)*. Geffen, 1994, compact disc.

Wigglesworth, Smith. *Greater Works: Experiencing God's Power*. New Kensington, PA: Whitaker House, 2000.

———. *Only Believe: Experiencing God's Miracles Every Day*. New Kensington, PA: Whitaker House, 1998.

Wilson, Julian. *Smith Wigglesworth: The Complete Story*. Milton Keynes: Authentic, 2011.

Wood, Roy, Jr., host. *Have I Got News for You*. Season 2, episode 1, "George Conway, Andy Richter." Aired Feb. 15, 2025, on CNN.

www.ingramcontent.com/pod-product-compliance
Lightning Source LLC
Chambersburg PA
CBHW052114090426
42741CB00009B/1803